KILLER PUZZLES.
Copyright © 2025 by St. Martin's Press. All rights reserved.
Printed in the United States of America.
For information, address St. Martin's Publishing Group,
120 Broadway, New York, NY 10271.

www.castlepointbooks.com

The Castle Point Books trademark is
owned by Castle Point Publishing, LLC.
Castle Point books are published and
distributed by St. Martin's Publishing Group.

ISBN 978-1-250-37300-7 (trade paperback)

Design by Noora Cox
Special thanks to Kate Riccio

Our books may be purchased in bulk for promotional, educational,
or business use. Please contact your local bookseller or the
Macmillan Corporate and Premium Sales Department at 1-800-221-7945,
extension 5442, or by email at MacmillanSpecialMarkets@macmillan.com.

First Edition: 2025

10 9 8 7 6 5 4 3 2 1

KILLER PUZZLES

Crosswords, Cyphers, Cryptograms, and More for the TRUE CRIME Obsessed

ARCHER THORNE

CASTLE POINT BOOKS
NEW YORK

CONTENTS

Serial Killers 9

Crimes of Passion 25

Spies and Assassins 41

Femme Fatales 57

Organized Crimes 75

Cult Killings 91

The Dark Side Of Fame 107

History-Making Cases 123

Shocking Stalkers 139

Mass Murderers 155

Solutions 171

You've watched the documentaries, listened to the podcasts, and read the books.

You know who done it, how they did it, and maybe even why they did it. But how well do you know the details of each case? Do you remember what everyday item gave the Grim Sleeper away? Or which serial killer wished he had gotten his real-estate license instead of committing atrocities? Would you know how to stop Ted Bundy in his tracks? Or how many female killers were nurses?

With over 120 ways to test your true-crime knowledge and flex your detective skills, *Killer Puzzles* is the mind-bending trivia book you've been waiting for. Each crossword puzzle, cryptogram, word search, matchup, scramble, and quiz includes little-known particulars, intriguing evidence, and fascinating forays into the minds of murderers. When it comes to history's most notorious criminals and their shocking crimes, there's no shortage of fatal facts to uncover and mysteries to solve.

SERIAL KILLERS

KILLER PUZZLES

TELLTALE HEARTS (AND OTHER THINGS)

Which killers were caught thanks to ordinary, everyday things?

ACROSS

5: Handcuffs on an escaped victim brought police to this cannibal's door.
6: This killer sent an "untraceable" floppy disk to police.
7: Parking near a fire hydrant got this killer caught.
9: This NYC rapist was tracked through a dating app.

DOWN

1: This creepy killer used letterhead to confess.
2: This charismatic killer was stopped for speeding in a stolen car.
3: This California killer was caught using DNA from his door handle.
4: His neighbors complained about clogged drains.
5: This psychopath was spotted using his victim's debit card at ATMs.
8: Discarding his pizza crust landed this predator in prison.

CONNECTING THE DOTS

Attackers leave behind DNA evidence in less than 10 percent of murders. Still, genetic genealogy has brought more than 600 murderers and rapists to justice since it was first used in the Golden State Killer's case.

KILLER MOVIES

A deranged killer makes for a great movie villain. Match the famous murderers to the movies they inspired.

1. *Monster*   A. **RICHARD RAMIREZ**
2. *Scream*   B. **ALAIN LAMARE**
3. *The Gray Man*   C. **JOHN WAYNE GACY**
4. *The Silence of the Lambs*   D. **HANNIBAL LECTER**
5. *Citizen X*   E. **JACK THE RIPPER**
6. *The Snowtown Murders*   F. **JOHN CHRISTIE**
7. *Psycho*   G. **TED BUNDY**
8. *10 Rillington Place*   H. **ED GEIN**
9. *Next Time I'll Aim for the Heart* I. **ALBERT FISH**
10. *To Catch a Killer*   J. **ALBERT DESALVO**
11. *The Night Stalker*   K. **RICHARD "DICK" HICKOCK**
12. *The Deliberate Stranger*   L. **DANIEL "DANNY" ROLLING**
13. *From Hell*   M. **JOHN BUNTING**
14. *In Cold Blood*   N. **AILEEN WUORNOS**
15. *The Boston Strangler*   O. **ANDREI CHIKATILO**

CURIOUS DETAIL

Jeffrey Dahmer has been the subject of at least twenty movies, shows, and documentaries—which is even more than Ted Bundy—as well as countless podcasts.

SERIAL KILLERS

KILLER PUZZLES

DAHMER'S REGRETS

This strangely wistful quote by convicted cannibal Jeffrey Dahmer hints at both his favorite hobby and the alternate career path he wished he'd followed.

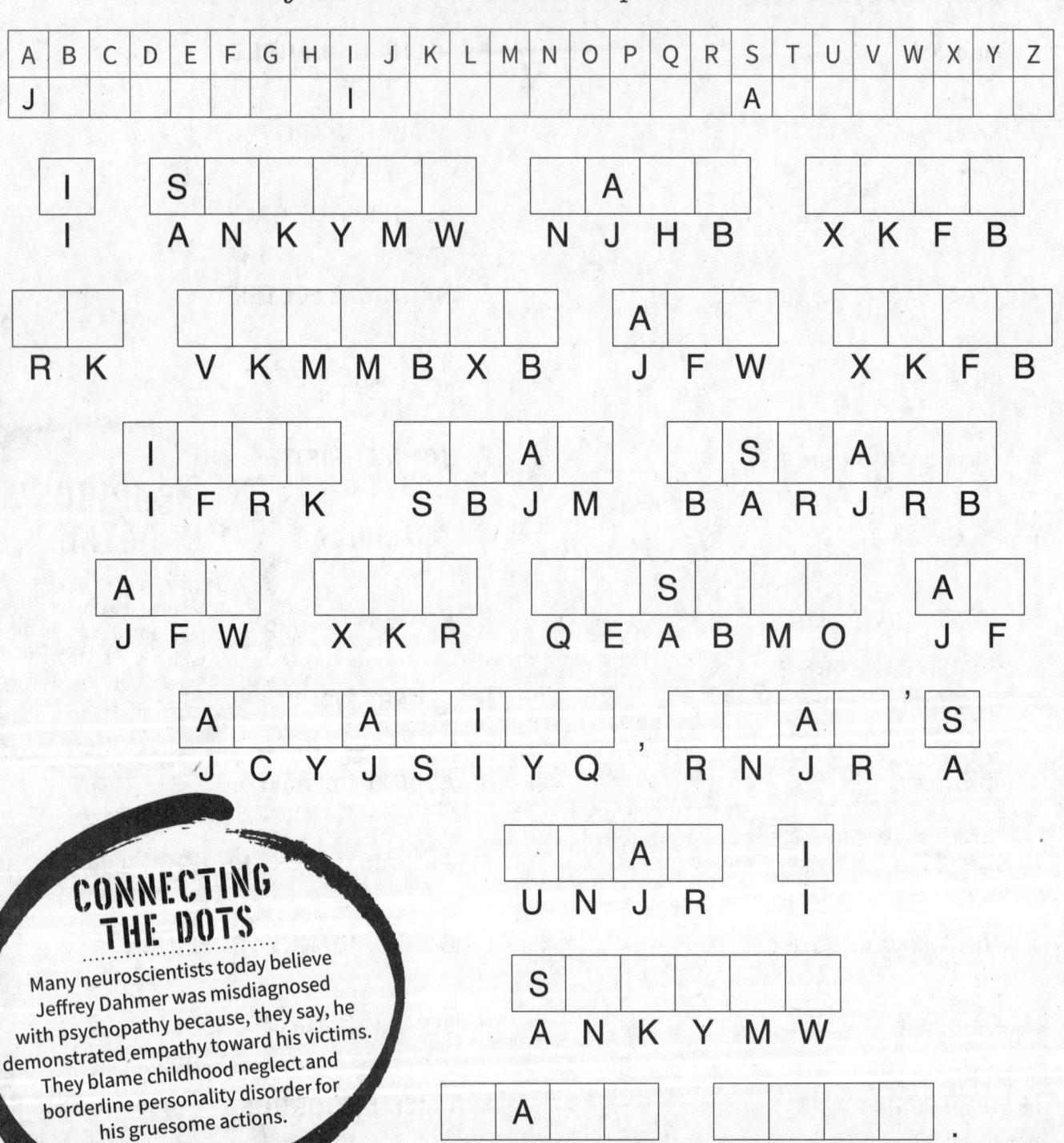

SERIAL KILLERS

TRUE-CRIME CATCHWORDS

Use your sleuthing skills to find these commonly used true-crime terms.

```
F E F S E N T E N C E Q R N
U V O P I Y Y S S E N T I W
G I R E L N T V L R E N V B
I T E M S Y M I P V Z G Q T
T O N T T A F A I L M Y D R
I M S L E O C D T A M Z Y D
V V I L R P E D N E I D T R
E U C P A N A H L B L L G D
G W S E C I U C I O B K M W
M N L E L N R L S N C R P W
J P N B T J A T R E V P Q Y
```

Profile	Fugitive	Alibi	Witness	Guilty
Forensics	Cold Case	Evidence	Escape	Trial
Motive	Manhunt	Plea	Inmate	Sentence

13

KILLER PUZZLES

NAMED, YET NEVER CAUGHT

Unscramble the fear-inspiring nicknames of killers who've yet to be caught.

1. The California killer who wrote letters to the editor.

   DZCOAI ELLIRK _____

2. The 1960s murderer who mostly preferred middle-aged women.

   OOTBSN NRSLGARTE _____

3. The man who raped and murdered seven in Detroit in the 1970s.

   TOIBFGO KLRIEL _____

4. The ruthless killer who haunted London, England.

   AKJC TEH RIPPRE _____

5. The southern slayer who turned lovers' lanes into nightmare fuel.

   ENAARKATX TAMHOPN RLKILE

   _____

6. The strangler who terrorized truck stops in Ohio.

   RD ON _____

7. The South African predator who used panties as a weapon.

   PELYES OOWHLL RELLKI _____

SERIAL KILLERS

8. The Japanese killer who kept to a calendar.

   YDSDENWAE ERLGNTRAS _____

9. The sketchy murderer with the innocent-sounding name.

   HET RDOOEDL _____

10. The monster who took children's lives in order.

    ETLBPAHA ILKELR _____

11. The butcher who targeted Native American women.

    HOMLKAOA CYTI CTUERBH _____

12. The sociopath who left victims in suggestive poses.

    MIIMA ELASGTRNR _____

13. The Florida man who used what he had on hand.

    DGOL CSKO ELIRKL _____

14. The killer who stabbed their way through Philadelphia in the late '80s.

    FRRFNKAOD HSRLEAS _____

CURIOUS DETAIL

Nicknames almost always originate with the press, but some come from investigators (similar to how Hannibal Lecter's "Buffalo Bill" in *Silence of the Lambs* started as a bad joke in Kansas City Homicide).

KILLER PUZZLES

MODUS OPERANDI

These men and women all had very particular habits and methods when it came to committing murder.

ACROSS

2: The cannibal who stocked his freezer with his victims' remains.
4: The murderer who inspired a manhunt by shooting into parked cars.
6: This nurse murdered up to sixty patients via lethal injection in Texas.
7: The killer who used a Volkswagen Beetle to lure victims.
8: Known as "the BTK Killer," he would bind, torture, and kill his victims.
9: This murderer found his victims through his construction company.
10: The infamous British doctor who injected up to 250 patients with heroin.

DOWN

1: The man arrested for allegedly burying his victims along Gilgo Beach.
3: This Chicago-based killer operated a "Murder Castle."
5: The killer who sent taunting letters to the police and press in San Francisco.

CONNECTING THE DOTS

Criminals are often creatures of habit, returning to the same modus operandi, or mode of operating, for each subsequent crime. Although a serial killer's MO may evolve, it will usually contain consistent characteristics that help authorities identify them and/or their victims.

BUNDY'S WORDS OF COMFORT

Ted Bundy provided this chilling rationalization when asked by journalists Hugh Aynesworth and Stephen Michaud if a killer might feel guilty. (Bundy would only answer hypothetical questions.)

A	B	C	D	E	F	G	H	I	J	K	L	M	N	O	P	Q	R	S	T	U	V	W	X	Y	Z
												Y													
														C											

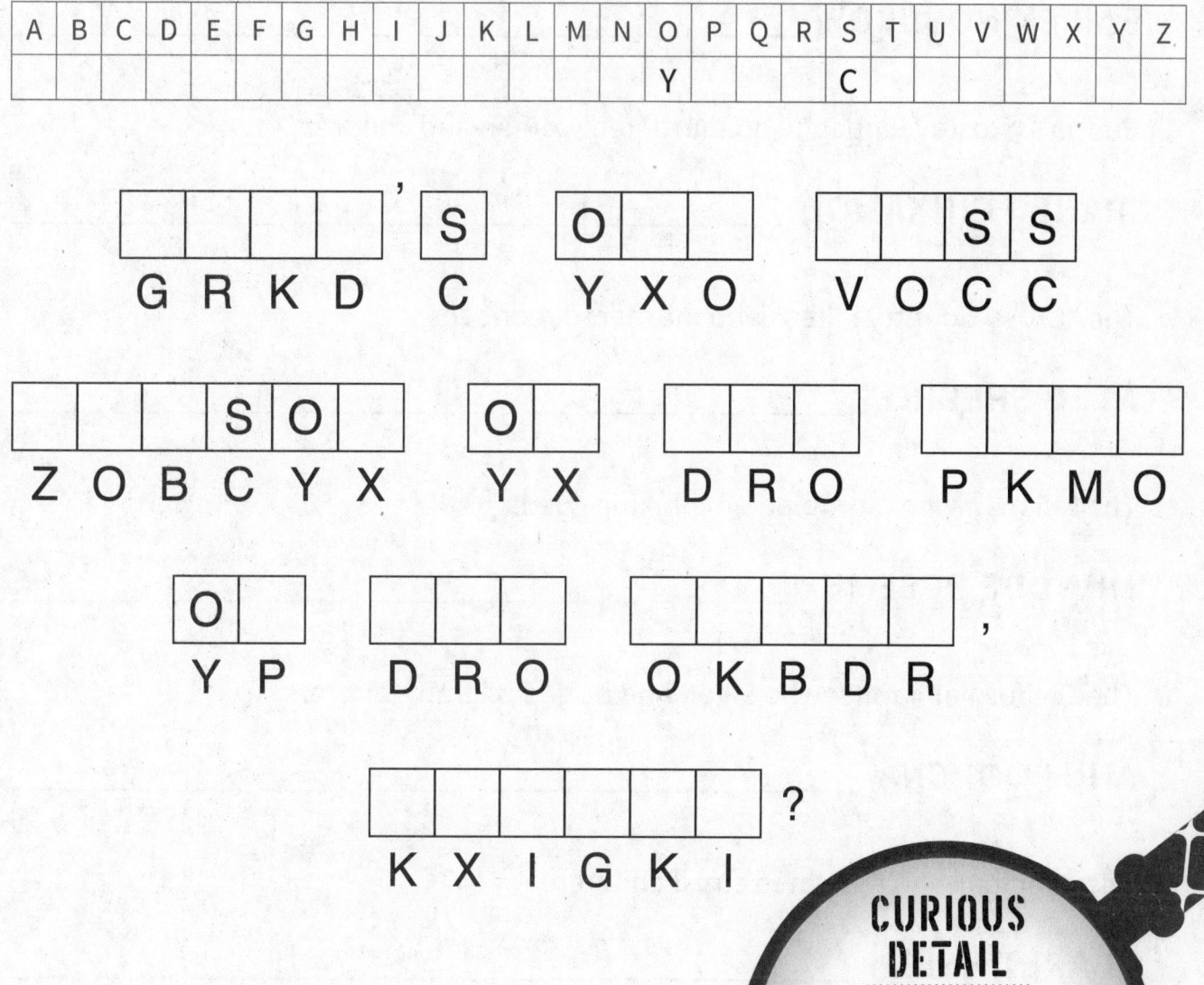

TERRIFYING KILLERS WITH A TYPE

Unscramble the names of these killers, who each targeted a specific type of victim.

1. The woman who robbed and killed her johns.

   EAILEN NOSUROW _____

2. Russia's "Rostov Ripper," who murdered women and children.

   IRANED CIHKATIOL _____

3. The "Cross-Country Killer" who murdered redheads.

   NLEG SREGRO _____

4. The tall man who murdered hitchhiking coeds.

   MUNDDE RPEEMK _____

5. The Californian farmer who killed and buried migrant laborers.

   ANUJ OORCNA _____

6. The cannibal who mutilated small children.

   LBARET HSIF _____

7. The "Death House Landlady" who murdered her elderly boarders.

   OAORHDTE ENPUTE _____

SERIAL KILLERS

8. The Norwegian killer who targeted alleged Marxists.

   DSANER KBRIEVI _____

9. The charmer who targeted brunettes with a middle part.

   EDT YNUBD _____

10. The Korean-Japanese businessman who murdered Western women in Tokyo.

    IJOJ ROABA _____

11. The Canadian killer who brought sex workers to his family's pig farm.

    BORTER KCPOTNI _____

12. The would-be photographer who murdered young women who modeled for him.

    NEYDRO LLACAA _____

13. The Alaskan killer who lured sex workers into the woods to hunt them.

    BETROR NASHEN _____

14. The East Coast angel of death who killed elderly hospital patients.

    SELRACH NCLULE _____

    _____

CONNECTING THE DOTS

Some killers have a type out of convenience (murdering elderly boarders for their Social Security checks, for example). But many (including a few on these pages) will murder people who resemble someone who hurt them, such as a former lover or an abusive parent.

19

KILLER PUZZLES

GACY'S RATIONALE

When asked by police about his unusual side hustle, John Wayne Gacy instilled a generation with coulrophobia by giving this simple justification.

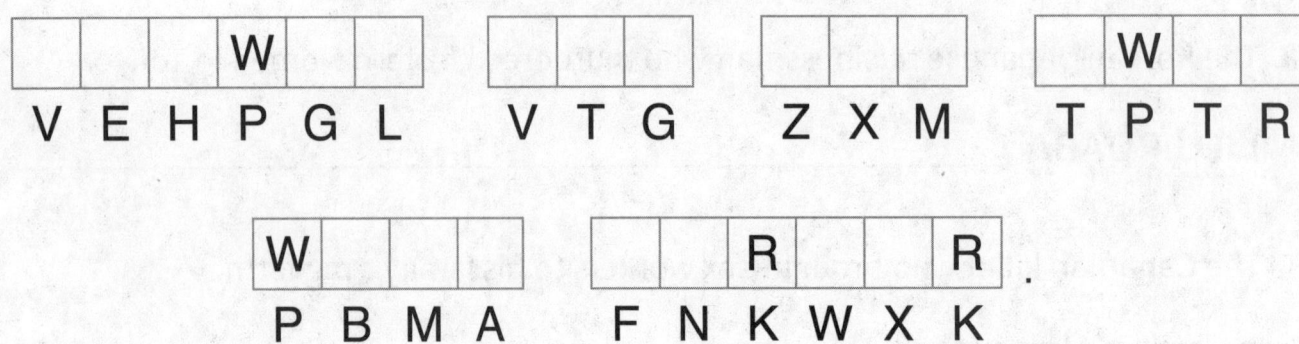

> **CURIOUS DETAIL**
>
> After being tortured and raped by Gacy, nineteen-year-old Robert Donnelly reported him to the police. The killer said the encounter was consensual, and the officers dropped the issue. By this point, Gacy had already buried several victims under his house.

THE MOST PROLIFIC AMERICAN KILLERS

These men have the notorious designation of most kills, with anywhere from eighteen to sixty murders under their belts.

```
E W C O R O N A N X G Y
U O N R L K D E N M C Y
Q O S T I G E I Y O V L
I D E E J D N A T L Z D
N F L V L O G T R K E N
I I W N B T I W Q N P R
M E O G E N T S A N E N
O L N Y G L E I T Y G Y
D D K H D Y S S L A N Z
G D A D C N V O N Q N V
R M P A Z L U P N A M O
R K G G B J Z B W W H Q
```

Little	Stano	Eyler
Ridgway	Nelson	Woodfield
Gacy	Kearney	Knowles
Corona	Bonin	Cottingham
Dominique	Bundy	Hansen

KILLER PUZZLES

STICKY ENDS

All but one of these killers died in prison, but none died of old age.
Match the murderer to the manner of their death.

1. John Wayne Gacy   A. ELECTRIC CHAIR
2. Earle Nelson   B. HANGED
3. Jeffrey Dahmer   C. LYMPHOMA
4. Ted Bundy   D. BREAST CANCER
5. Larry Eyler   E. SUICIDE BY HANGING
6. Paul John Knowles   F. COMPLICATIONS OF AIDS
7. Charles Ray Hatcher   G. COMPLICATIONS OF COVID-19
8. Robert Pickton   H. SHOT BY INVESTIGATORS
9. Arthur Shawcross   I. MYSTERIOUS DEATH IN CELL
10. Peter Sutcliffe   J. CARDIAC ARREST WOUND
11. Richard Ramirez   K. BEATEN BY A FELLOW PRISONER
12. Joseph Christopher   L. SPEARED BY A FELLOW PRISONER
13. Herb Baumeister   M. LETHAL INJECTION
14. Nannie Doss   N. SELF-INFLICTED GUNSHOT
15. Lonnie Franklin, Jr.   O. LEUKEMIA

CURIOUS DETAIL

Here's a hint: The one man on this list who didn't die in a cell was nicknamed "the Casanova Killer." He escaped police custody and went on a four-month crime spree across state lines and sent recorded confessions to an attorney before his death.

KILLER RECALL

Test your true-crime knowledge with a quick chapter quiz.

1. Where did John Wayne Gacy typically find his victims?
   _____

2. What led police to discover Dennis Nilsen's dirty secret?
   _____

3. What do authorities believe was behind Jeffrey Dahmer's dark proclivities?
   _____

4. Do most serial killers change up their methods?
   _____

5. What disease did in Nannie Doss?
   _____

6. How did the Zodiac Killer taunt police?
   _____

7. What did Ted Bundy believe he had to offer police?
   _____

8. How many women make the list of the top fifteen American serial killers?
   _____

9. Which movie did Albert Fish's crimes inspire?
   _____

10. Why did Dorothea Puente murder her victims?
    _____

CRIMES OF PASSION

KILLER PUZZLES

IN THE HEAT OF THE MOMENT

Who committed these notorious crimes of passion?

ACROSS

3: The killer convicted for the brutal murder of her boyfriend, Travis Alexander, in a jealous rage.

7: The South African Olympian who fatally shot his girlfriend, Reeva Steenkamp, claiming mistaken identity.

8: This man was convicted of murdering his pregnant wife, Laci, in what was initially believed to be a missing person case.

9: The brothers who shot their wealthy parents in their Beverly Hills home in 1989, citing years of abuse as their motivation.

10: The central figure in the Long Island Lolita case, this man's teenage lover, Amy Fisher, shot his wife in the head.

DOWN

1: This Hollywood actor was acquitted of killing his wife, Bonny Lee Bakley, but was found liable in a civil case.

2: The dentist who ran over her cheating husband with her car in anger.

4: The Arizona man who murdered his wife and two children before setting their house on fire.

5: The New York native murdered her ex-husband and his new wife after a bitter divorce.

6: The victim of a famous assault by his wife, Lorena, who claimed years of abuse.

CURIOUS DETAIL

Crimes of passion often involve perpetrators acting out of intense emotional responses, such as jealousy or betrayal, and using readily accessible means to do so. This is what made the Long Island Lolita case particularly shocking—Amy Fisher used a revolver to shoot her target in the face at point-blank range.

TWISTED TOOLS

Match these offenders to their particular methods.

1. Michael Peterson
2. Tiffany Hall
3. Darlie Routier
4. Susan Smith
5. Lorena Bobbitt
6. Robert Fisher
7. Christopher Watts
8. Cameron Hooker
9. Diane Downs
10. Nathaniel Bar-Jonah
11. Karla Homolka
12. Jodi Arias
13. Lori Vallow
14. James Holman
15. Richard Speck

A. DRUG OVERDOSE
B. KIDNAPPING AND CANNIBALISM
C. POISON
D. KNIFE AND GUN
E. DISPOSAL IN AN OIL FIELD
F. STRANGULATION AND STABBING
G. DISMEMBERING
H. RAPE AND STRANGULATION
I. SHOOTING WITH A REVOLVER
J. BEATING
K. IMPRISONMENT IN A BOX
L. DROWNING
M. STABBING WITH A KNIFE
N. BLUNT FORCE TRAUMA
O. ARSON (HOUSE FIRE)

CONNECTING THE DOTS

In the infamous Cameron Hooker case, he kept his victim, Colleen Stan, confined in a wooden box under his bed for seven years, using psychological manipulation and fear tactics to control her. At Cameron's trial, Stan's experience was cited as unprecedented in the history of the FBI.

CRIMES OF PASSION

KILLER PUZZLES

LORENA'S REASONING

Many men took Lorena Bobbitt's attempt on her husband's manhood as seriously as murder. She gave this rationale for disposing of his penis in an open field.

A	B	C	D	E	F	G	H	I	J	K	L	M	N	O	P	Q	R	S	T	U	V	W	X	Y	Z
			K												P										

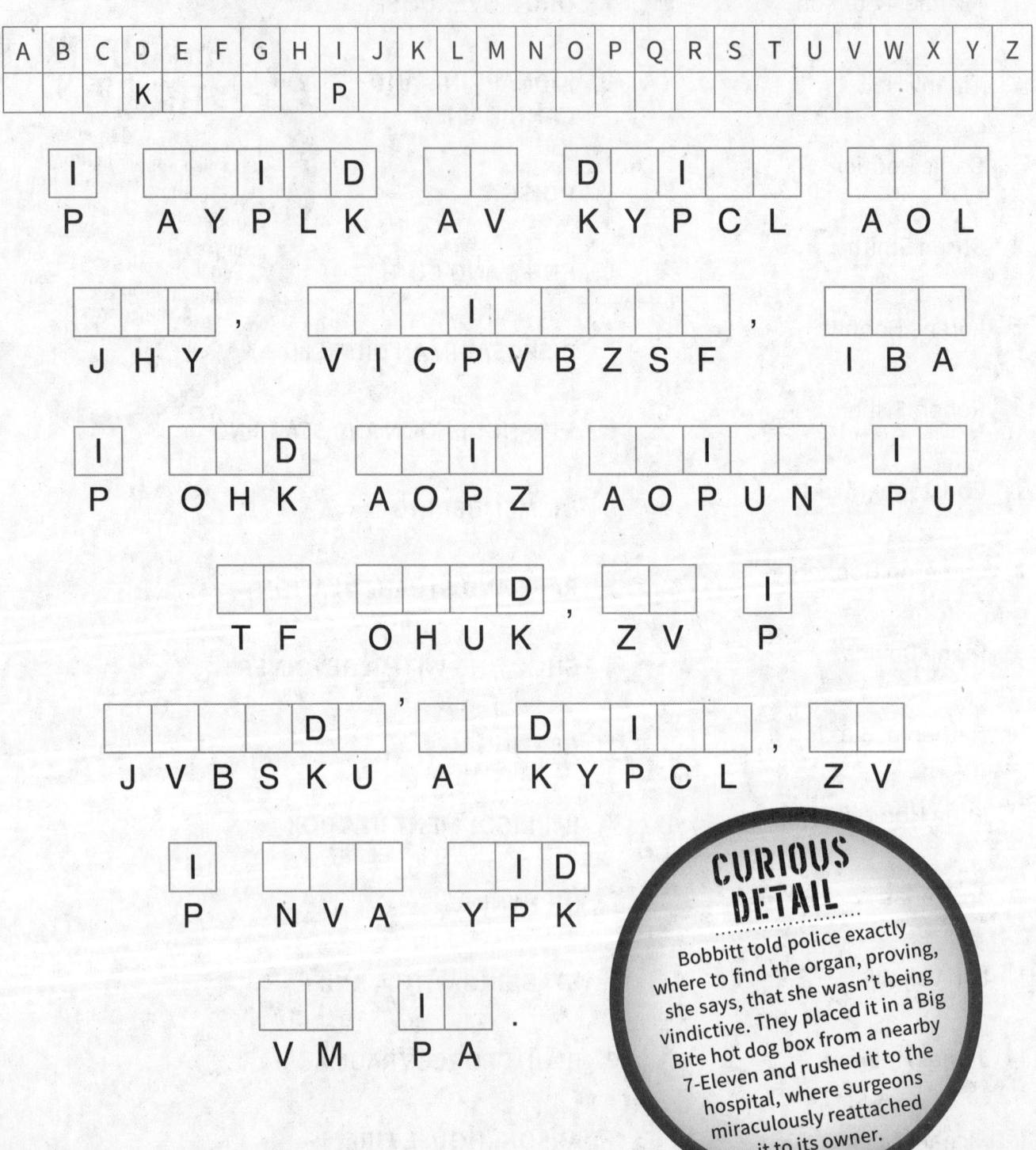

CURIOUS DETAIL

Bobbitt told police exactly where to find the organ, proving, she says, that she wasn't being vindictive. They placed it in a Big Bite hot dog box from a nearby 7-Eleven and rushed it to the hospital, where surgeons miraculously reattached it to its owner.

HOW TO CATCH A KILLER

Uncover the many techniques and clues police use to nab a murderer.

```
N O I T A G O R R E T N I
F D C X P R S T I N G S M
S I T O L O T S P R U V Y
C M N E N J L G E R W H W
I T B G S F Q Y V N A P L
S S N D E T E E G I T Y T
N A L I Y R I S R R S I L
E L R M R L P M S P A D W
R I M E L P A R O I Y P Y
O V R A M L T T I N O Y H
F A N R I A U O N N Y N L
K C L B W A C D O X T Y N
E Z I Y L Y Q Y T F W B T
```

- Surveillance
- Fingerprint
- Saliva
- Hair
- Witness
- Confession
- Sting
- Cameras
- Alibi
- Forensics
- Polygraph
- Autopsy
- Footprint
- Testimony
- Interrogation

CRIMINAL CONFESSIONS

Unscramble the names of murderers who have confessed to their crimes.

1. He confessed to killing over thirty women across the United States in the 1970s.

   EDT DYBUN _____

2. A Mafia hitman who confessed to involvement in nineteen murders and turned state's witness.

   ASMYM ANOARVG _____

3. Following the brutal Chicago murder of eight student nurses, this killer confessed in 1966.

   HCIRDAR EKPSC _____

4. Houston mother who confessed to drowning her two children in a bathtub in 2016.

   BRAHOEHS STOAMH _____

5. Soviet serial killer who confessed to murdering over fifty women and children.

   RDIEAN LITKAICHO _____

6. Along with his brother, he confessed to the murder of their wealthy parents.

   EYLL ZENDEEMN _____

7. The South African Olympian who confessed to fatally shooting his girlfriend.

   AORSC RSTPIIUSO _____

CRIMES OF PASSION

8. She confessed to murdering her ex-boyfriend in the shower.

   IODJ SRAIA _____

9. She admitted to killing seven men in Florida while working as a prostitute in the late 1980s and early 1990s.

   ENILAE NORSOUW _____

10. The Scottish serial killer who confessed to a series of child murders in the 1960s.

    NIA YRDAB _____

11. Known as "the Killer Clown," this murderer confessed to killing more than thirty young men.

    OHJN NYAWE AYCG _____

12. After his wife went missing for nearly forty years, this killer finally pleaded guilty to manslaughter.

    MIALWIL ZRONOK _____

13. Often referred to "the Green River Killer," this felon confessed to killing forty-nine women.

    RAYG AYDIGWR _____

14. This woman confessed to poisoning her husband and son using antifreeze.

    IDAEN DETUTSA _____

> **CONNECTING THE DOTS**
>
> Henry Lee Lucas, the self-proclaimed "Confession Killer," confessed to over 600 murders beginning in the 1980s, but was only convicted of murdering 11 people. Decades after his confessions, DNA testing revealed he had lied about killing at least 20 people.

KILLER PUZZLES

LETHAL LOVE TRIANGLES

Which killers acted out of jealousy?

ACROSS

7: This woman developed an intense jealousy toward her sixteen-year-old ward, Sylvia Likens, torturing and mutilating her in 1965.

8: This headmistress of a private school in Virginia made headlines for killing her longtime lover after learning of his affair with a younger woman.

9: This killer conspired with her teenager lover, Billy Flynn, to murder her husband and continue their affair.

CURIOUS DETAIL

Jealousy and betrayal in a romantic relationship have proven to be major motivators for murder; globally, more than 35 percent of all murders of women are reported to be committed by an intimate partner.

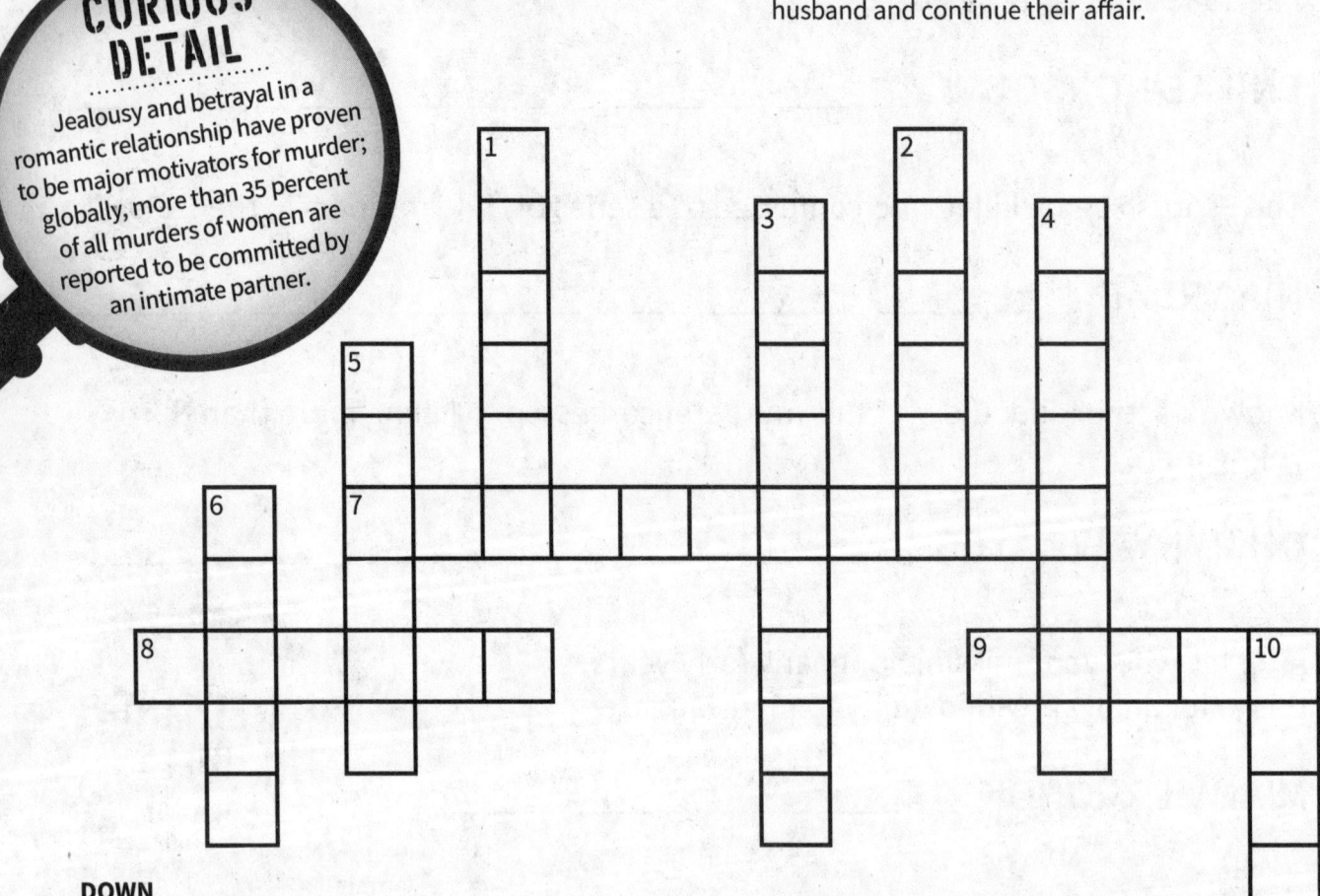

DOWN

1: In 2008, this Florida woman was convicted of murdering her husband, Larry, after he discovered her ongoing affair and planned to leave her.

2: This former schoolteacher was convicted of murdering her lover's wife, Betty Jeanne Solomon, in a fit of jealousy.

3: After years of bitter divorce proceedings, this New York native murdered her ex-husband and his new wife in 1989.

4: In 2016, this convict killed her lover's partner, Sadie Hartley, in England.

5: In this 2012 Kentucky case, this woman shot and killed her on-again, off-again boyfriend, Ryan Poston.

6: This Texas woman conspired with her lover, Tracey Tarlton, to kill her millionaire husband so they could inherit his wealth.

10: In what became known as the "Trial of the Century," this millionaire shot and killed architect Stanford White on the roof of Madison Square Garden.

HUBERS'S EXPLANATION

This is the comment Shayna Hubers made during a police interview when asked about the gunshot wound she inflicted on her boyfriend's face.

A	B	C	D	E	F	G	H	I	J	K	L	M	N	O	P	Q	R	S	T	U	V	W	X	Y	Z
E																						A			

I **GAVE** **HIM**
M KEZI LMQ

THE **NOSE** **JOB** **HE**
XLI RSWI NSF LI

ALWAYS **WANTED**.
EPAECW AERXIH

CONNECTING THE DOTS

Though she initially claimed the murder was self-defense, Hubers soon began incriminating herself on the phone with the 911 operator. She reasoned that Poston was going to die anyway and was twitching to the point where she couldn't watch him anymore, justifying her six shots.

MAINTAINING THEIR INNOCENCE

Unscramble the names of convicts who refused to confess to their alleged crimes.

1. This convicted rapist and serial killer spent twenty-nine years in prison before confessing to six of his murders in 2007.

   WARDDE RUTSART _____

2. The notorious Australian serial killer who inspired the horror film *Wolf Creek* never confessed to any of the seven murders he was convicted of.

   VINA IALTM _____

3. Though this twenty-seven-year-old was executed for the 1983 murder of gas station employee Wanda Lopez, he maintained his innocence.

   SRACLO NUAEDL _____

4. This man maintained his innocence when convicted of murder and kidnapping in 1992 and 1996; DNA evidence exonerated him in 2002.

   YRA NRKEO _____

5. In the case that inspired *The Fugitive*, this doctor was convicted of murdering his pregnant wife but never admitted guilt; after a decade in prison, he was retried and released.

   MSA DPSHPEAR _____

6. This man admitted to participating in a 1975 shootout but maintained that he did not kill the FBI agents he was convicted of murdering.

   DALROEN ETLIERP _____

7. One of the "West Memphis Three," this man was convicted of triple homicide in 1993, maintaining his innocence until his 2011 release in a plea deal.

   IMADEN SHEOCL _____

CRIMES OF PASSION

8. Convicted of murdering seven men in 1989 and 1990, this woman maintained that the killings were self-defense.

   IANELE SOWNURO _____

9. The *Serial* podcast revolved around this man's murder of his ex-girlfriend, which he denies.

   NANAD YDSE _____

10. Accused of murdering her roommate during a study abroad semester in Italy, this subject of the 2007 case was convicted twice before being fully exonerated in 2015.

    MDANAA OXKN _____

11. Though he was sent to prison in 2004 for murdering his pregnant wife, this convict publicly claimed his innocence as recently as 2024.

    TCSOT OSPTRNEE _____

12. This former doctor and US Army captain was convicted in 1979 of murdering his pregnant wife and two daughters, yet he maintained his innocence.

    FJEYFER NDLCAMDAO _____

13. Often referred to as "the Green River Killer," this felon finally confessed to killing forty-nine women only after the FBI appealed to his ego.

    RAYG AYDIGWR _____

14. He was jailed for murdering his wife despite maintaining that she fell down the stairs.

    HLEIAMC SOETENRP _____

    _____

CURIOUS DETAIL

According to the Innocence Project, 25 percent of wrongful convictions overturned by DNA evidence result from a false confession, which can arise from coercive interrogation tactics, among other factors.

KILLER PUZZLES

HUNTLEY'S MANIPULATION

This is the emotional statement Ian Huntley made to the media after murdering two young girls, Holly Wells and Jessica Chapman, in 2002.

A	B	C	D	E	F	G	H	I	J	K	L	M	N	O	P	Q	R	S	T	U	V	W	X	Y	Z
										K									T						

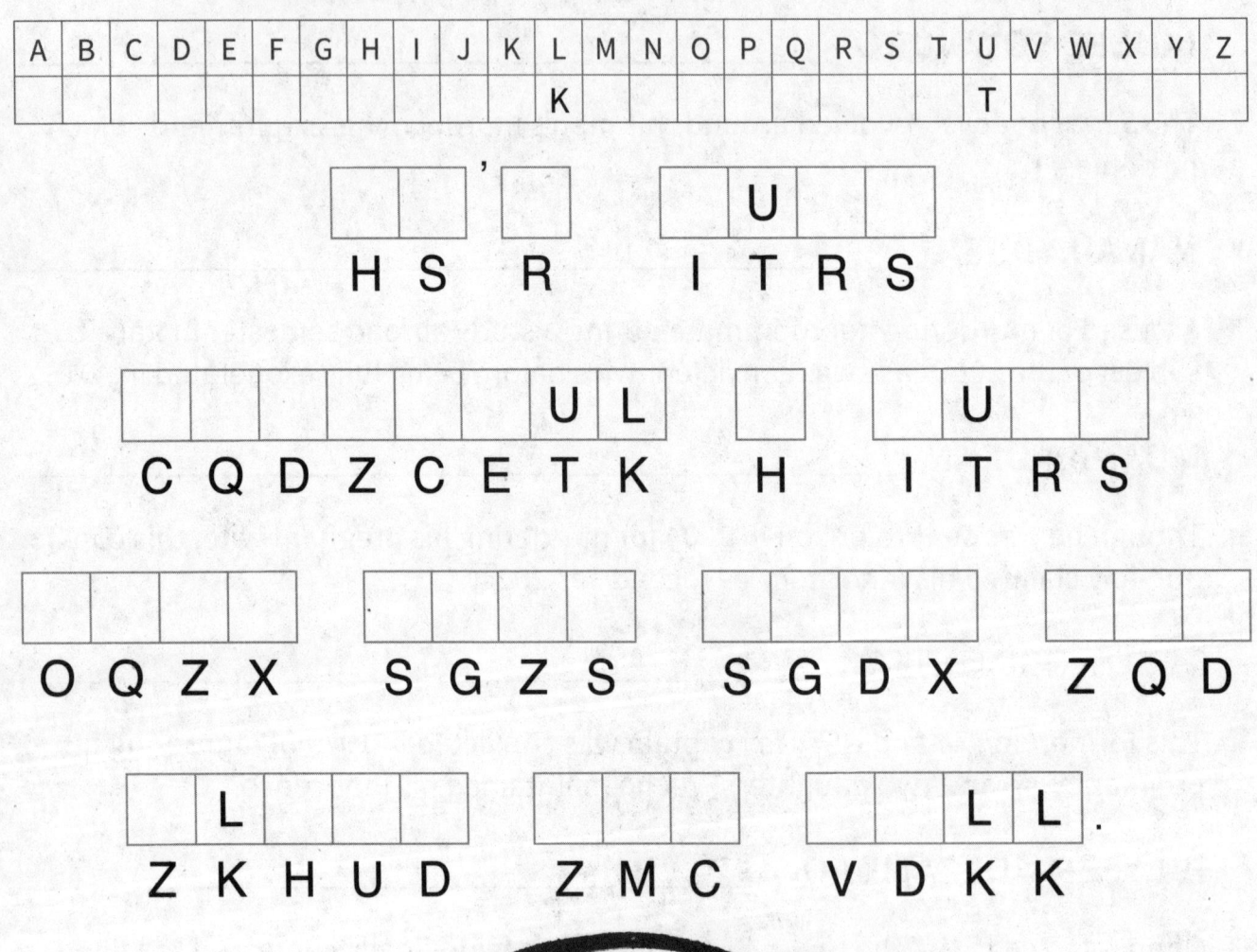

CONNECTING THE DOTS

While the community desperately searched for the missing girls and reeled from their disappearances, Huntley expressed concern as well. He participated in search efforts and confidently feigning his innocence—actions that made the case all the more chilling.

CRIME SCENE ESSENTIALS

Uncover the items authorities bring to crime scenes.

```
T L U M I N O L N N K
E H L M B X Y Q S I S
W P G Y A R S K T A K
R C A I S R E M M J S
D X A T L T K P R G B
G A I M C H L E A O R
L K P H E E S B R D F
O V E E S R L A R S P
V S P B T N A O L Q M
E J A L D O N Y R F V
S D T P Y E N D T J Q
```

Tape	Kit	Samples
Markers	Tape	Forms
Camera	Flashlight	Kits
Notepad	Gloves	Sketches
Bags	Luminol	Drone

NOTORIOUS COORDINATES

Match each notorious criminal to the location where their crimes took place.

1. John Wayne Gacy
2. Ed Gein
3. Jesse Pomeroy
4. Richard Ramirez
5. Zodiac Killer
6. Robert Hansen
7. Dennis Rader
8. David Berkowitz
9. Jack the Ripper
10. Dale Hausner
11. Paul Bernardo
12. Lyle and Erik Menendez
13. Aileen Wuornos
14. James Holmes
15. Gary Ridgway

A. CENTRAL FLORIDA
B. ANCHORAGE, ALASKA
C. SEATTLE, WASHINGTON
D. SCARBOROUGH, ONTARIO
E. AURORA, COLORADO
F. PLAINFIELD, WISCONSIN
G. WHITECHAPEL, LONDON
H. SAN FRANCISCO, CALIFORNIA
I. WICHITA, KANSAS
J. BEVERLY HILLS, CALIFORNIA
K. LOS ANGELES, CALIFORNIA
L. PHOENIX, ARIZONA
M. CHICAGO, ILLINOIS
N. NEW YORK CITY, NEW YORK
O. BOSTON, MASSACHUSETTS

CONNECTING THE DOTS

As of 2024, New York is the US state with the most known serial killers in history, topping the list with eighteen documented killers. California is not far behind, though, recording fifteen serial killers convicted. Of course, many notorious criminals escaped to other areas of the country to avoid getting caught.

KILLER RECALL

Test your true-crime knowledge with a quick chapter quiz.

1. What was the nickname of the killer who falsely claimed to have murdered 600 people?

2. What weapon did Amy Fisher use in the Long Island Lolita case?

3. In what state did Robert Hansen murder his victims?

4. True or false: After his case went viral on the *Serial* podcast, Adnan Syed admitted to killing his ex-girlfriend.

5. Though he was found guilty of her murder, how does Michael Peterson insist his wife died?

6. To whom did Shayna Hubers accidentally admit she shot her boyfriend?

7. What did the Menendez brothers claim was the motivation for their crimes?

8. Which state has the most documented serial killers in history?

9. Where did Lorena Bobbitt dispose of her husband's penis?

10. How many women did Gary Ridgway confess to killing?

SPIES AND ASSASSINS

KILLER PUZZLES

SHOTS AT THE OVAL

Name the assassins who attempted to kill a US president—some successfully.

ACROSS

4: He fired five bullets at Franklin Delano Roosevelt, missing his target but fatally wounding four people, including Chicago's mayor.

6: This man shot Theodore Roosevelt during a campaign speech, though the former president survived.

9: He ended President William McKinley's life in 1901 at the Pan-American Exposition.

10: He was infamously linked to John F. Kennedy's 1963 Dallas motorcade.

CONNECTING THE DOTS

In 1912, Theodore Roosevelt survived an assassination attempt while delivering a speech. Roosevelt famously continued his speech for another 50 minutes after the attempt—with the bullet lodged in his chest.

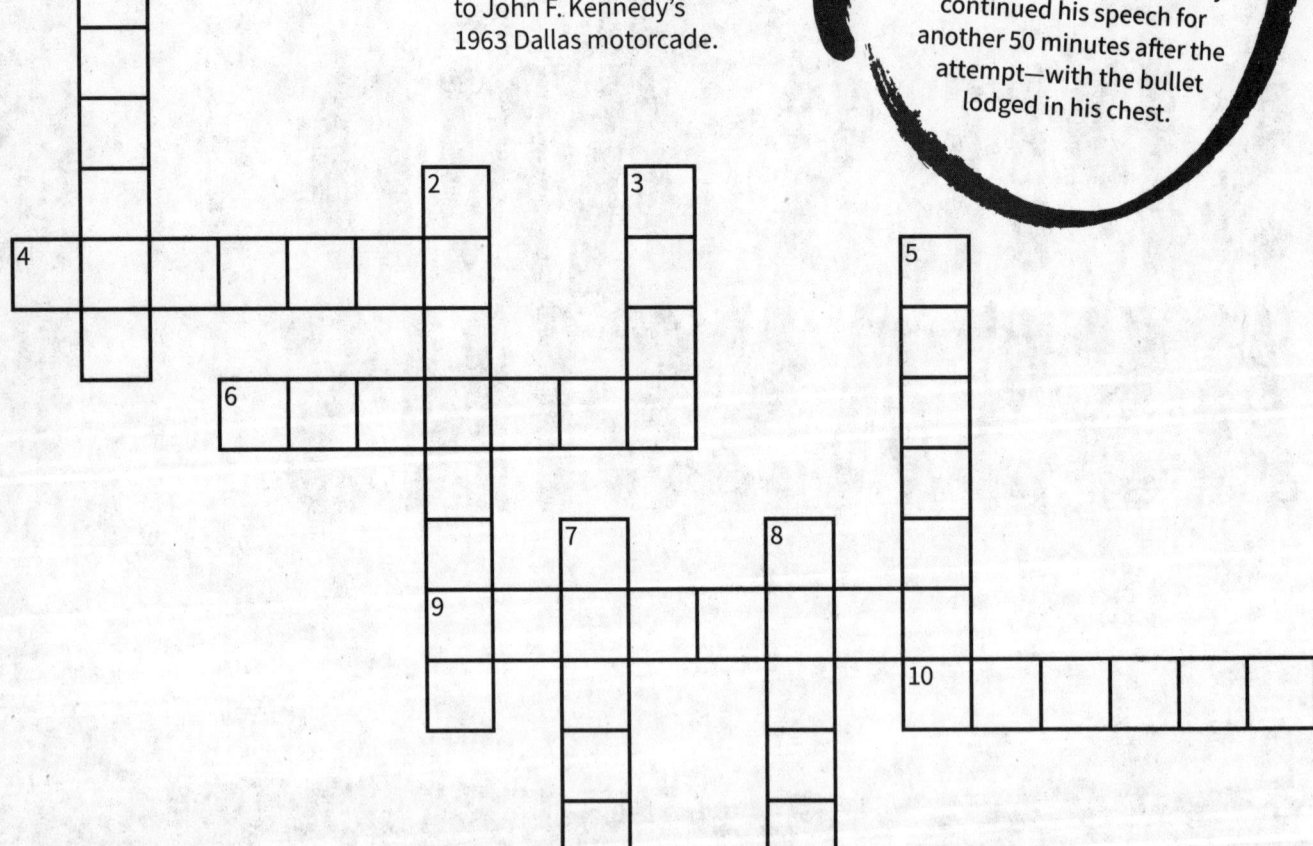

DOWN

1: This man assassinated President James Garfield in a train station.

2: Considered the first known person to attempt the assassination of a sitting US president, he tried to shoot Andrew Jackson, but both pistols misfired.

3: He tried to hijack a plane to crash into Richard Nixon's White House.

5: One of the two Puerto Rican nationalists who attempted to kill Harry Truman in 1950.

7: The man behind Abraham Lincoln's fateful night at Ford's Theatre.

8: The woman who fired at Gerald Ford in 1975 but missed.

CELEBRITY TARGETS

Match the criminal to the high-profile star they assassinated or attempted to assassinate.

1. Mark David Chapman
2. Charles Manson
3. Valerie Solanas
4. Andrew Phillip Cunanan
5. Arthur Richard Jackson
6. Kevin James Loibl
7. Yolanda Saldívar
8. William Ragland
9. Trevor Charles Howell
10. Michael Abram
11. Günter Parche
12. Hells Angels members
13. Ehsanullah Ehsan
14. Lester Lloyd Coke
15. Daryl Baum

A. GEORGE HARRISON
B. THERESA SALDANA
C. MICK JAGGER
D. PAUL PIERCE
E. SHARON TATE
F. MALALA YOUSAFZAI
G. 50 CENT
H. GIANNI VERSACE
I. MONICA SELES
J. JOHN LENNON
K. FRANK ZAPPA
L. BOB MARLEY
M. CHRISTINA GRIMMIE
N. ANDY WARHOL
O. SELENA

CURIOUS DETAIL

American actress and activist Theresa Saldana was attacked in 1982 by her stalker. The high-profile case brought significant attention to the dangers of stalking. Following her recovery, Saldana advocated for stronger anti-stalking laws and increased awareness of the risks faced by victims.

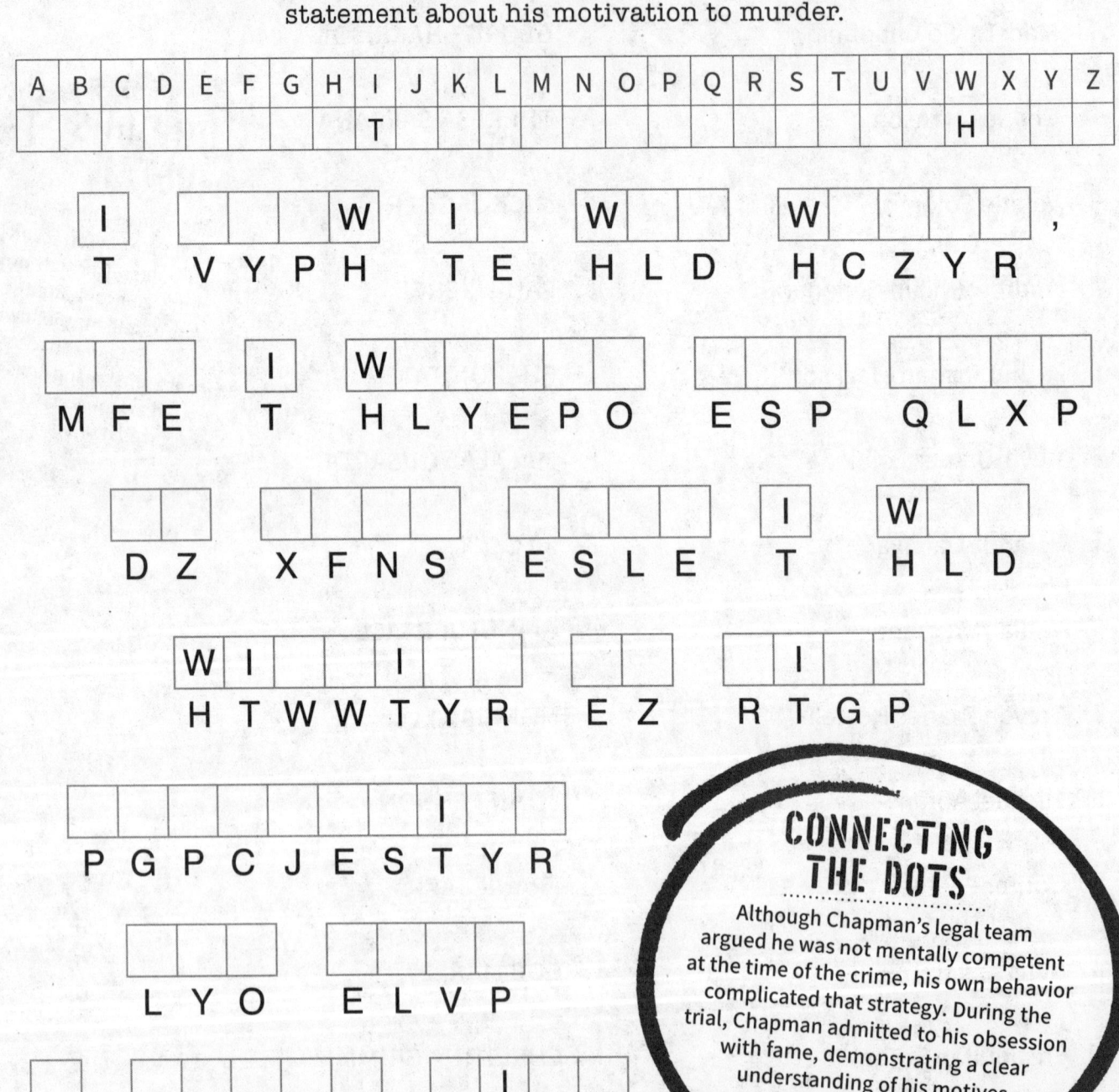

SPIES AND ASSASSINS

ESPIONAGE HOT SPOTS

Find the names of the famous locations where notable spies and assassins have been caught.

```
Y T I C K R O Y W E N W
M E X I C O C I T Y A G
G Y V J A D H B A S V Y
T N D R W N E A H B J P
E A I N D R N I V M U A
L M Q J L K N E O A V D
A R N I I G O S I E N P
V E N O T E C K N V A A
I G B O D O B E G R J D
V W N W W N G R I N L G
R D Z D J Z O S V X A L
C B P D N P M L J V Y B
```

Berlin	Vienna	New York City
Moscow	Beijing	Geneva
Washington DC	Havana	Bangkok
London	Germany	Mexico City
Paris	Tel Aviv	Dubai

45

SECRET AGENT SCRAMBLE

Using the hints, unscramble the letters below to reveal the names of these famous spies.

1. During World War II, this German theoretical physicist was an infamous double agent, known for leaking atomic secrets.

   UASKL SUCFH _____

2. This Soviet intelligence officer defected to the West and revealed the identities of multiple Soviet spies in the United Kingdom.

   GELO SKYDROVIEG _____

3. Known for her role as a Dutch exotic dancer, she was convicted of infiltrating high levels of the US government by spying for Germany.

   AMTA IRHA _____

4. As part of the Cambridge Five, this British spy worked for the KGB, betraying his colleagues by divulging British secrets to the Soviets.

   IMK BPIYHL _____

5. This American was a notorious spy for the Soviet Union during the Cold War, known for revealing numerous US intelligence secrets.

   TBORER SENSHNA _____

6. A Russian-born aerospace engineer, he was a high-ranking pilot in the Soviet Union who defected to the United States in a supersonic fighter jet.

   KOIVRT ENKBEOL _____

   _____

CURIOUS DETAIL

Studies estimate that during the Cold War, US spy agencies recruited around 1,000 former Nazis to work as informants for America, illustrating the extensive network of spies at the time.

SPIES AND ASSASSINS

7. This American naval officer was arrested for spying on behalf of the Soviet Union and selling US secret information during the Cold War.

   OHNJ RELAWK _____

8. This Spanish spy served as a German double agent during World War II, operating under the alias "Agent Garbo" and playing a vital role in the D-Day deception.

   ANUJ UOLPJ ACRGAI _____

9. While working undercover as a German journalist, this man was a key figure in espionage activities during World War II, primarily in Japan.

   RDCIRHA RGOSE _____

10. This South Korean businessman was convicted of spying for North Korea.

    MIK GNOD-UHLC _____

11. A longtime CIA officer turned Soviet mole convicted for espionage in 1994.

    RAIDLHC SMEA _____

12. This former US State Department employee was sentenced to life in prison in 2010 after spying for Cuba for nearly thirty years.

    DENLKLA SMRYE _____

13. This Israeli spy was involved in high-profile missions; after leaking nuclear secrets, he was convicted of espionage.

    HTAJOANN LADROLP _____

14. A notorious KGB operative in the United States, this woman was arrested in 2010 as part of the Illegals Program.

    NAAN PAANMHC _____

KILLER PUZZLES

UNDERCOVER OPERATIONS

Identify the historical espionage operations hinted at in the clues.

ACROSS

7: (2 wds.) The British intelligence network of five high-profile agents who passed secrets to the Soviets during the Cold War.

8: (2 wds.) The explosion of a US munitions depot orchestrated by the Germans in 1916 that caused massive destruction and pushed the US closer to World War I.

10: NATO's secret Cold War program that was organized to form stay-behind armies in case of a Soviet invasion in Europe.

CONNECTING THE DOTS

Many major espionage operations strained international relationships, as certain covert missions revealed deep-seated mistrust between allies and enemies alike. This ultimately shaped decades of diplomatic tensions and led to the escalation of conflicts like the World War II and the Cold War.

DOWN

1: A CIA mission to recover a Soviet submarine in the Pacific Ocean during the Cold War.

2: A British operation that used a corpse with fake documents to deceive the Nazis about Allied invasion plans during World War II.

3: A telegram from the Germans that proposed an alliance with Mexico but was intercepted by the British during World War I.

4: A political scandal involving a break-in at Democratic National Committee headquarters.

5: (2 wds.) The US Navy's covert operation to tap Soviet underwater communication cables during the Cold War.

6: A US counterintelligence program that decrypted Soviet communications.

9: The joint American and British Cold War operation to build a tunnel underneath Berlin for the purpose of intercepting Soviet communications.

PHILBY'S RATIONALIZATION

Kim Philby, a spy for the Soviet Union and member of the Cambridge Five spy ring, denied betraying his country in the following comment.

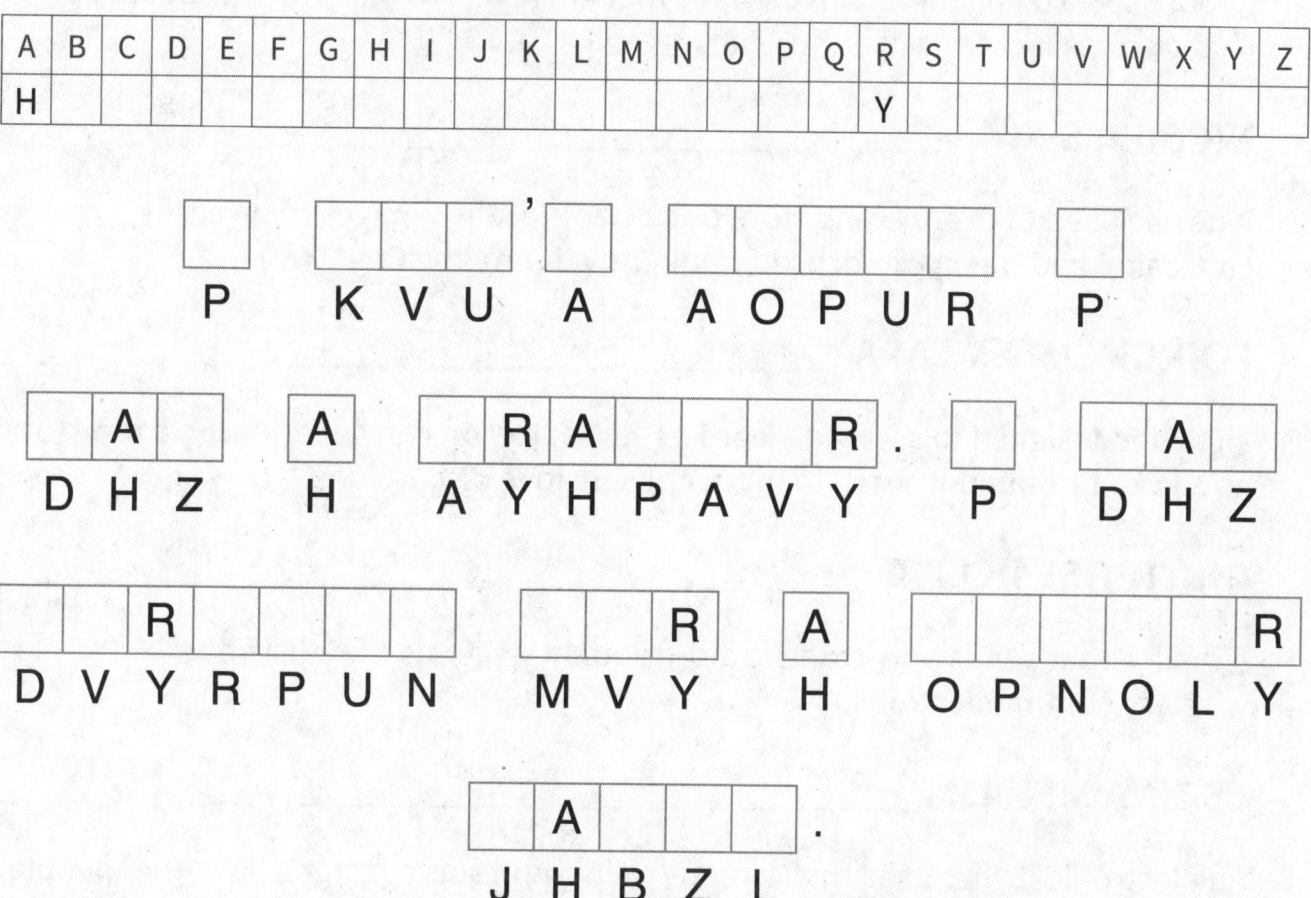

CURIOUS DETAIL

Though he was eventually caught and exonerated for divulging British secrets to the Soviet Union, Philby evaded detection for more than thirty years. His double life was so convincing that he continued to rise through the ranks of British intelligence.

DECODING SPY GADGETS

Unscramble the equipment that helps spies get the job done.

1. A tool used to send discreet messages that are revealed only when exposed to heat or certain chemicals.

   NIEBIIVLS KNI _____

2. A device used to capture and store documents as tiny images to be easily concealed and transported; used frequently during the Cold War.

   FOIRCMLMI EMCARA _____

3. A gadget designed to secretly record or eavesdrop on conversations in a room or phone call; commonly used to intercept sensitive discussions.

   GINITENSL DEEIVC _____

4. A device that sends out strong radio-frequency signals that disrupt wireless communications.

   LSGINA MERAJM _____

5. An electronic device used to discreetly follow and survey targets, whether people or vehicles.

   SGP ACRTRKE _____

6. A device that emits a dense smoke screen used to create a distraction or aid in an escape.

   MKOSE BOBM _____

7. A location set up to intercept and monitor communications, often used to gather information from afar.

   NESTILNGI SPOT _____

8. A device or software that records keystrokes on a computer or keypad to collect passwords and confidential data.

   KEGYRGLOE _____

9. A light-emitting device that can also capture video, ideal for nighttime surveillance.

   FSIHTGHLAL AMCRAE _____

10. A portable storage device that can encrypt files to prevent unauthorized access and is used for secure data transport.

    RIVENASUL ALISER SUB _____

11. A weapon disguised within common objects or clothing, allowing for surprise use and ideal for self-defense or stealthy attacks.

    DIHNDE FNKIE _____

12. An audio-recording device hidden in ordinary objects to capture sound.

    ERNCPOMOIH _____

13. A functional writing instrument that also records video, ideal for discreet surveillance.

    NEP AEAMCR _____

14. Eyewear that amplifies light or uses infrared light to create a visible image in low-light conditions.

    NHTIG IOVINS GLESOGG _____

CONNECTING THE DOTS

Modern spies often use covert listening devices that are small enough to fit into everyday objects like light switches, smoke detectors, or alarm clocks. These devices transmit audio for long periods of time, allowing spies to gather plenty of information without blowing their cover.

KILLER PUZZLES

HASENFUS'S REALIZATION

Eugene Hasenfus, who was involved in the Iran-Contra affair, made this self-aware statement about the dangerous reality of being entangled in an operation of its magnitude.

I KNEW TOO MUCH, AND THAT MADE ME A LIABILITY. SOMETIMES, KNOWING THE TRUTH IS MORE DANGEROUS THAN LIVING IN IGNORANCE.

CURIOUS DETAIL
Investigations after Hasenfus's capture led to a significant political scandal. Despite maintaining that he didn't have detailed knowledge of the covert actions, President Reagan issued a public apology in 1987.

NOTABLE TARGETS

From political figures to musicians, these high-profile victims were assassinated in highly controversial and public cases.

```
M E K O O C Y W G X J R
C N L O C N I L G Q M Q
K D M A L C O L M X M T
I L G Y T N N E G Y R J
N E Z V D R O A V O D M
L I W S Y E N T T E N M
E F A Y O D N S W O R R
Y R L E H G K N N E J S
G A L I Y Y L N E G N J
Q G A K T A E O N K R J
B R C Y P L G I Z W W T
Q M E G W N K T Q C R Z
```

Gandhi	McKinley	Evers
Trotsky	Garfield	Newton
Lennon	Kennedy	Czolgosz
Malcolm X	King, Jr	Wallace
Lincoln	Cooke	Gaye

THE ESPIONAGE NETWORK

Match each spy title to its job description.

1. Double Agent
2. Mole
3. Sleeper Agent
4. Handler
5. Courier
6. Asset
7. Spy Master
8. Surveillance Operative
9. Cryptanalyst
10. Saboteur
11. Intelligence Analyst
12. Cutout
13. Provocateur
14. Defector
15. Field Agent

A. INCITES ILLEGAL ACTS
B. PROVIDES INTEL
C. BETRAYS THEIR COUNTRY
D. DISRUPTS ENEMY OPS
E. MONITORS TARGETS
F. SECURES INFO EXCHANGES
G. DECODES MESSAGES
H. GATHERS INTEL
I. LEADS A NETWORK OF SPIES
J. OVERSEES FIELD AGENTS
K. LEAKS INTEL
L. WORKS BOTH SIDES
M. DELIVERS SECRET MESSAGES
N. INTERPRETS DATA
O. ACTS WHEN ACTIVATED

CONNECTING THE DOTS

During the Cold War, the CIA planned to use cats as spies for their project Operation Acoustic Kitty. They hoped to spy on Soviets through microphones and transmitters implanted in cats, but the project failed due to the test cat's unpredictable nature.

SPIES AND ASSASSINS

KILLER RECALL

Test your true-crime knowledge with a quick chapter quiz.

1. Which US president was the victim of the first attempted assassination?

2. The public became more aware of the dangers of stalking after the attempted assassination of which American actress?

3. What did Mark David Chapman claim was his motive for killing John Lennon?

4. True or false: It is estimated that during the Cold War, spy agencies recruited around 1,000 former Nazis to spy for America.

5. What scandal involving covert ops led to the first US presidential resignation?

6. How long did Kim Philby evade detection as a spy for the Soviet Union and member of the Cambridge Five?

7. True or false: President Reagan initially admitted he had detailed knowledge of the operation of the Iran-Contra affair that led to scandal.

8. Which Spanish spy had the nickname "Agent Garbo" and served as a German double agent during World War II?

9. What operation did the CIA develop that involved bugging animals?

10. What is the title for a spy who oversees field agents?

FEMME FATALES

KILLER PUZZLES

MOMMY DEAREST

Which murderous moms committed these heinous crimes?

ACROSS

4: The Italian soap maker who murdered her neighbors to bring her sons good luck.

7: The English nurse convicted for the deaths of four children in the 1990s.

9: A Canadian accomplice in the murders of teenage girls alongside her husband.

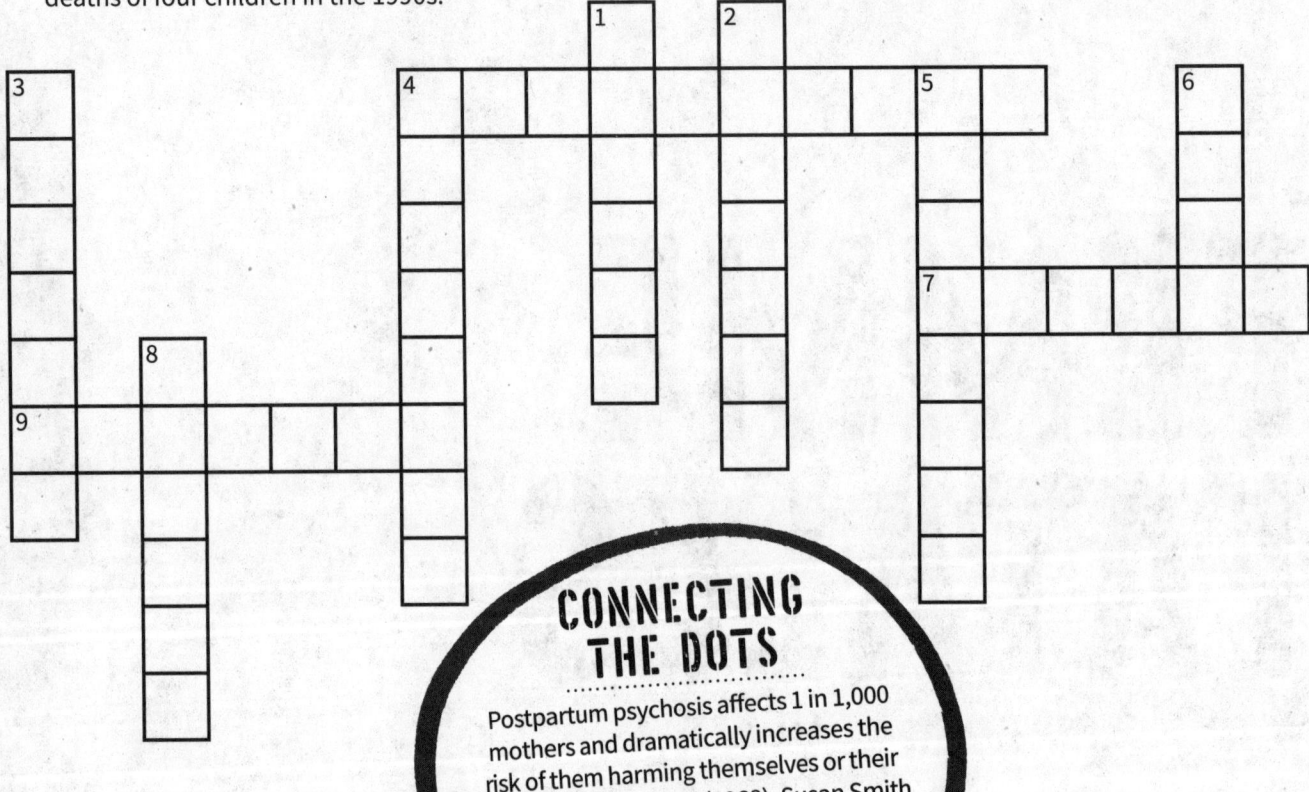

CONNECTING THE DOTS

Postpartum psychosis affects 1 in 1,000 mothers and dramatically increases the risk of them harming themselves or their children. Waneta Hoyt (1968), Susan Smith (1994), Andrea Yates (2001), and Carol Coronado (2014) are just a few sufferers who took their children's lives during psychotic episodes.

DOWN

1: The Australian woman sentenced to life without parole for a horrific act of revenge on her partner.

2: The New York woman whose nine children died from a variety of suspicious deaths.

3: The British mom of two who stabbed men while they walked their dogs.

4: The woman whose husband stood by her after she stabbed their three daughters to death.

5: The notorious New Orleans socialite whose shocking cruelty to enslaved people made history.

6: The American woman who smothered her five infants because she couldn't stand them crying.

8: Nicknamed "the Black Widow," this Colombian drug lord ordered hundreds of murders.

A KILLER, BY ANY OTHER NAME...

Match these women to their murderous monikers.

1. Barbara Graham
2. Nannie Doss
3. Miyuki Ishikawa
4. Aileen Wuornos
5. Sara María Aldrete
6. Elizabeth Báthory
7. Frances Knorr
8. Linda Hazzard
9. Martha Wise
10. Gesche Gottfried
11. Dorothea Puente
12. Leonarda Cianciulli
13. Juana Barraza
14. Beverley Allitt
15. Mariam Soulakiotis

A. BLOOD COUNTESS
B. DAMSEL OF DEATH
C. LADY OF SILENCE
D. SOAP-MAKER OF CORREGGIO
E. GIGGLING GRANNY
F. BLOODY BABS
G. MOTHER RASPUTIN
H. ANGEL OF DEATH
I. ANGEL OF BREMEN
J. DEATH HOUSE LANDLADY
K. LA MADRINA
L. BABY FARMING MURDERESS
M. BORGIA OF AMERICA
N. STARVATION DOCTOR
O. DEMON MIDWIFE

FEMME FATALES

CURIOUS DETAIL

More than 300 witnesses pointed to Elizabeth Báthory when officials were investigating rumors that the noblewoman had been killing young girls to use their blood as a beauty treatment.

KILLER PUZZLES

WUORNOS'S STRANGE END

This bizarre phrase, sprinkled with a smattering of movie references, was among Aileen Wuornos's last words on this earth.

A	B	C	D	E	F	G	H	I	J	K	L	M	N	O	P	Q	R	S	T	U	V	W	X	Y	Z
				Z														N							

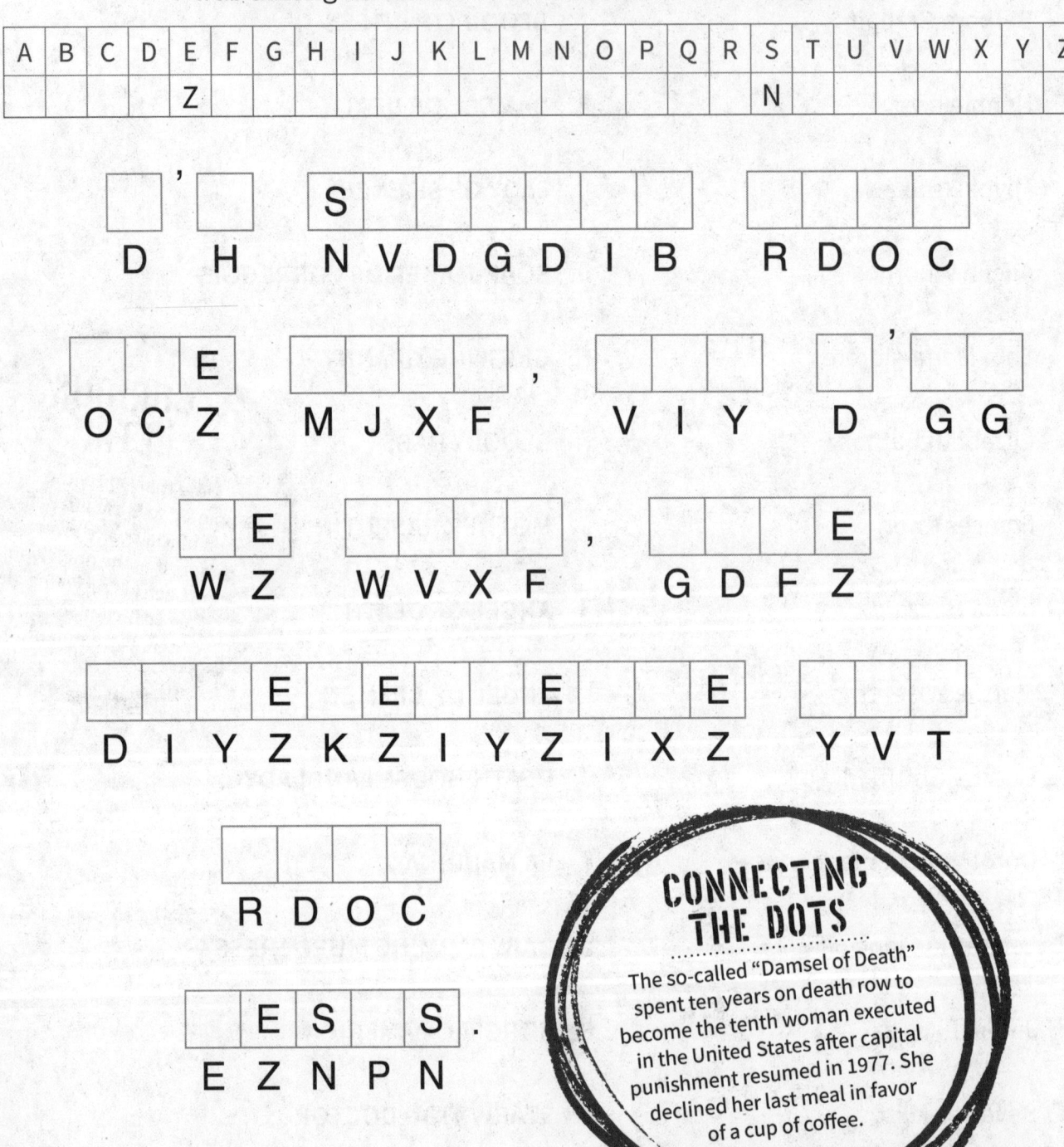

CONNECTING THE DOTS

The so-called "Damsel of Death" spent ten years on death row to become the tenth woman executed in the United States after capital punishment resumed in 1977. She declined her last meal in favor of a cup of coffee.

FLIRTING WITH MURDER

Find the female killers who flew under the radar long enough to rack up multiple kills.

```
D N A P P O T M P O N G R
E W J Y W P B T N Q Y N M
I L E N B B R A N G J Z P
R A Y T W H O M O L K A D
F L Z X T N G I L B E R T
T A K A E L W N D T E T S
U W U R U A E Z Y T S Z
O R B P O R N U B Y E P K
G I B R E N A R F N U L Y
P E N Y E T E B N E I J N
L O D H M V J U N M R Z D
S R Y N O L G T E N N T R
D N D Y P B E K Z N J Y T
```

Wettlaufer
Gilbert
Wuornos
Puente
Barraza
Homolka
Dennehy
Buenoano
LaLaurie
Dyer
Toppan
Gottfried
Klimek
Overbye
Gunness

GOODNIGHT NURSE

Unscramble the names of history's most famous Angels of Death.

1. The VA hospital nurse convicted of administering lethal doses of epinephrine to four patients.

   KTSREIN ILTBERG _____

2. This nineteenth-century nurse said she wanted to kill more people than anyone else.

   JNAE NATPOP _____

3. The British nurse who killed four children under her care in the early 1990s.

   VERBEEYL LTAILT _____

4. This Victorian-era "baby farmer" was hanged for murdering infants in her care.

   LAMIEA DREY _____

5. The Canadian nurse who confessed to killing eight elderly patients by injecting them with insulin.

   ALEIZBHTE EFTLTAUERW _____

6. The West Virginia nursing assistant convicted for injecting seven veterans with lethal doses of insulin.

   ETRA SAMY _____

7. This Texas nurse killed five dialysis patients by injecting bleach into their IV lines.

   MBREILKY CLRAK ASENZ _____

FEMME FATALES

8. The British neonatal nurse who murdered several infants between 2015 and 2016.

   YULC YTBEL _____

9. The Finnish nurse who was convicted of killing five elderly patients by poisoning.

   NOAI KNPOYP-KISOK _____

10. This Italian nurse was accused of killing patients who annoyed her by administering lethal doses of potassium chloride.

    LAINEDA AGPGOILI _____

11. This Texas nurse was convicted of killing infants by injection in the 1980s.

    NEEGNE JOSNE _____

12. The ringleader of a group of Austrian nurses, who together, killed at least forty-nine elderly patients.

    DRAULWTA RAGNEW _____
    _____

> **CURIOUS DETAIL**
> Murder in the medical field isn't a strictly female phenomenon. Male nurses Charles Cullen, Donald Harvey, Colin Norris, Michael Swango, and Niels Högel killed dozens of patients (and more than a few coworkers).

13. The conwoman whose "fasting cure" starved her clients to death.

    NDIAL ZDZAHRA _____

14. The woman who murdered elderly patients in a Michigan nursing home as part of a twisted love pact.

    DONYWLGNE GMARHA _____

63

ARSENIC AND OLD LACE

Which killers had a proclivity for poisoning their victims?

ACROSS

1: Considered the first British female serial killer, she poisoned around twenty-one people.

3: India's first convicted female serial killer, who used cyanide to kill her robbery victims.

6: The French servant and serial killer who poisoned up to thirty-six people with arsenic.

7: She poisoned seventeen family members and killed three after being forced to end her relationship.

8: The mom who poisoned her ex's oatmeal, then strangled him with his favorite tie.

10: The seventeenth-century Italian woman who sold poison to 600 unhappy wives.

CONNECTING THE DOTS

Female serial killers tend to use more discreet methods (like poison) than men and target family members, the elderly, and the ill, making them more likely to escape detection for longer.

DOWN

2: The notorious nurse who confessed to over thirty murders, including at least one strychnine poisoning.

4: The ancient Greek wife who poisoned her husband, the emperor.

5: The first woman executed after capital punishment was reinstated in 1976 for using rat poison to kill at least four.

9: The twentieth-century black widow who poisoned four husbands with rat poison.

METHODS OF MURDER

Track down the tools used by famous murderesses.

```
S L O T S I P D B S L L Y
C E R I N J E C T I O N R
K A V D P W H A M M E R R
N C R I A I R D K F I R E
S B I T S V L N D P W G N
L H E P A O I L O P Z X N
L R O T E F L I O E Z D D
I V I V E C S P P W G R N
P O Y X E O I O X L W J N
N Z G Y N L R J G E M Z L
```

Poison	Ice Pick	Pills
Pistol	Pillow	Shovel
Hammer	Fire	Starvation
Rope	Water	Injection
Car	Knife	Explosives

BLACK WIDOWS

Unscramble the names of these spouse-slaying killers.

1. This "Giggling Granny" used arsenic to eliminate her husband and son for insurance money.

   ANNINE SSDO _____

2. This widow attempted to blow up her last fiancé for a $100,000 insurance payout.

   DYUJ OANEBONU _____

3. The nineteenth-century "Angel of Bremen" was known for poisoning fifteen people with arsenic.

   CESEHG FOTGTRDIE _____

4. This Chicago widow who claimed to foresee the deaths of her victims but was later found guilty of poisoning them.

   ILTILE EKILMK _____

5. The infamous Connecticut nursing home operator who inspired the play *Arsenic and Old Lace*.

   MAY HCRARE-GILGLNIA _____

6. The oldest woman on North Carolina's death row, she poisoned her husband and boyfriend with arsenic.

   CHALNBE OTYLAR OMERO _____

7. This Canadian murderer, known as "the Torso Killer," inspired a musical with her name in the title.

   LEEYVN ICDK _____

FEMME FATALES

8. The "Merry Widow of Windy Nook" who murdered four husbands using insecticide.

   RYMA TBIEALZHE WNLISO _____

9. The Texas woman executed in 2000 for killing two husbands; she buried one under a wishing well.

   YETBT OLU ETBES _____

10. The Australian psycopath who skinned and cooked her boyfriend.

    EHKATRINE NGITHK _____

11. The early twentieth-century Norwegian-American serial killer who was notorious for murdering suitors on her farm.

    LELBE NNSGUES _____

12. This widow waited until two decades after her divorce to kill her first husband (though all five died under mysterious circumstances).

    TBYET UMANER _____

13. The New York woman who poisoned her husbands with antifreeze and tried to frame her daughter.

    EYCTAS AOTCSR _____

    _____

14. The "Black Widow of Kyoto" who was convicted of using cyanide to kill her husbands in Japan.

    KSICHOA HAKIKE _____

    _____

CURIOUS DETAIL

The fate of serial killer Belle Gunness remains a mystery to this day. When her home burned down in 1908, authorities found the decapitated body of a woman in the rubble. But without forensics, they had no way of proving it belonged to the murderess.

KILLER PUZZLES

MURDER FOR MONEY

Which female killers were in it for the profits?

ACROSS

2: This Australian serial killer poisoned her husband and children for the life insurance money in the late 1800s.

5: The British serial killer who, alongside her husband, killed tenants and sold their belongings.

6: The "Queen of Poisoners" who used various lethal substances to kill multiple family members for inheritance in the mid-twentieth century.

7: The Japanese black widow who poisoned partners for millions in insurance payouts.

8: The Dutch serial killer who poisoned 102 people and killed 27 to benefit from their funeral insurance in the late 1800s.

9: The famous nineteenth-century baby farmer who collected fees to care for infants she then killed.

CONNECTING THE DOTS

Female serial killers are rarer than their male cohorts, committing one in six of all serial murders. More than half of those accounted for murdered children, and a quarter targeted the elderly and infirm.

DOWN

1: The Sacramento landlady who murdered tenants for their Social Security checks.

3: This nineteenth-century German serial killer poisoned employers for financial security.

4: Sentenced to execution, this North Carolina woman poisoned several relatives and others from whom she'd stolen money.

5: The British "Merry Widow" who killed multiple husbands for their estates.

ATKINS'S SOLUTION

What did the Manson family murderess give as her reason for killing actress Sharon Tate?

A	B	C	D	E	F	G	H	I	J	K	L	M	N	O	P	Q	R	S	T	U	V	W	X	Y	Z
						B		D																	

___ ___ ___ ___ _ _ G G I G _ ___ ___ ___
CZ   F Z K O   W Z B B D I B   V I Y

___ ___ ___ ___ ___ ___ I ___ G ___ ___ ___
 K   G   Z   V   Y   D   B   V   I   Y

___ ___ ___ ___ ___ ___ I ___ G ___ ___ ___
 K   G   Z   V   Y   D   B   V   I   Y

___ _ _ G G I G_ , ___ ___ ___ I
 W Z B B D I B   V   I   Y   D

G ___ ___   ___ I ___   ___ ___
  B J O   D X F   J A

___ _ _ _ I _ G _ ___ ___ ___ ___ ___ , ___ ___
G D N O Z I D I B   O J   C Z M   N J

I ___ ___ ___ ___ ___ ___ ___ ___.
  D   N O V W W Z Y   C Z M

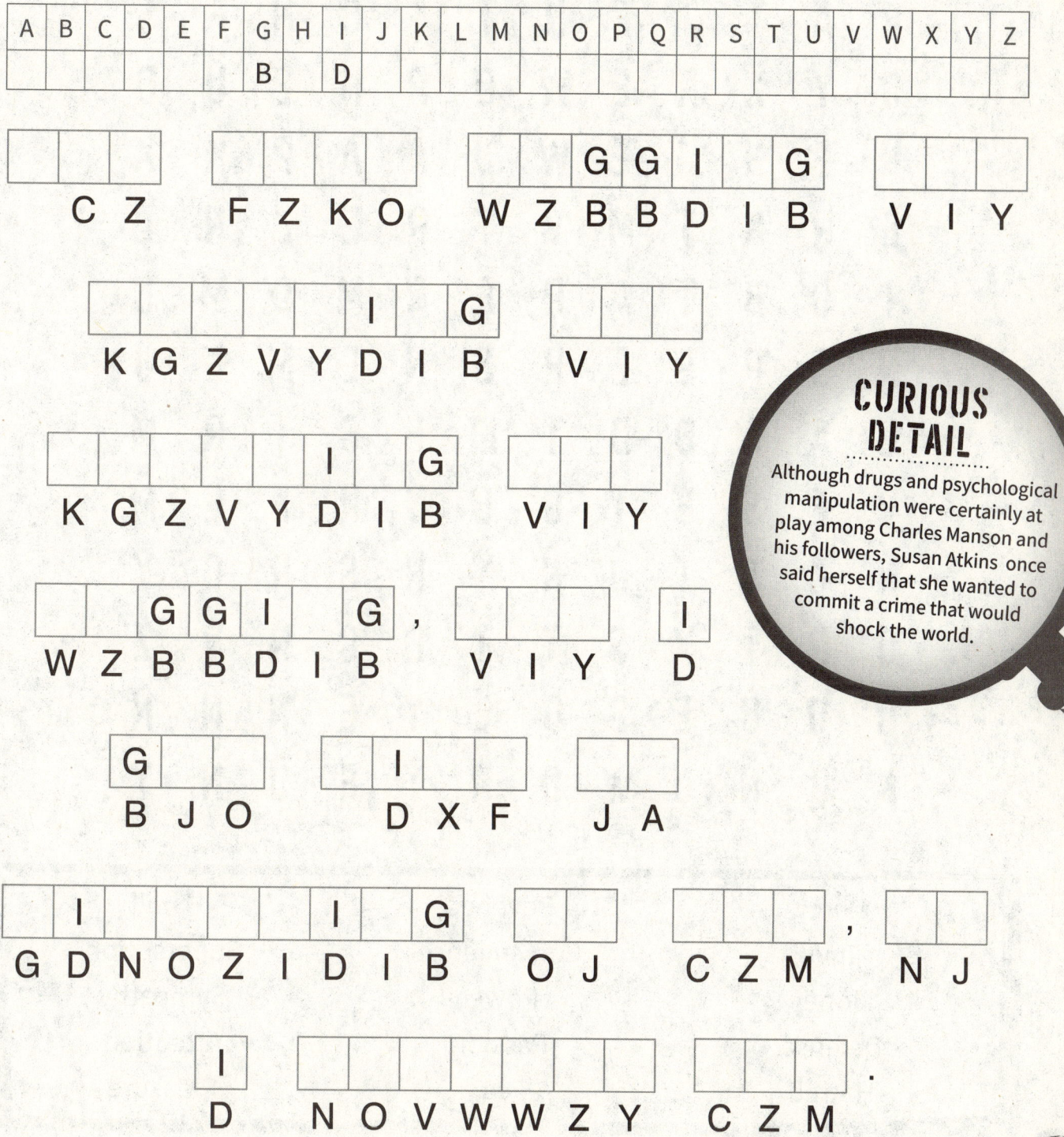

CURIOUS DETAIL

Although drugs and psychological manipulation were certainly at play among Charles Manson and his followers, Susan Atkins once said herself that she wanted to commit a crime that would shock the world.

KILLER PUZZLES

MOTIVES FOR MURDER

Tap into the minds of murderers to uncover these common motives.

```
E A T T E N T I O N F S
C Y X R E W O P H E U D
N E H J E W J A A P K X
E R K T M V T R E J N L
I U B T A R E R M D M L
N S P L E P S N E M L J
E A A D D T M F G I R M
V E S B I G E Y R E E M
N L S T J N Y H S R O Y
O P I X S T T D C N V Z
C O O E B Q L Y E N N N
N Q N J W D R Y E J N Y
```

Mercy	Revenge	Thrill
Envy	Convenience	Superstition
Money	Power	Sympathy
Defense	Passion	Attention
Hatred	Fear	Pleasure

FEMME FATALES

PARTNERS IN CRIME

Match these killers to their accomplices.

1. Karla Homolka
2. Martha Beck
3. Sara María Aldrete
4. Myra Hindley
5. Rosemary West
6. Gwendolyn Graham
7. Lila Young
8. Joanna Dennehy
9. Lavinia Fisher
10. Mary Bell
11. Amelia Sach
12. Carol Bundy
13. Bonnie Parker
14. Barbara Graham
15. Catherine Birnie

A. CLYDE BARROW
B. PAUL BERNARDO
C. WILLIAM YOUNG
D. JACK SANTO
E. DOUG CLARK
F. FRED WEST
G. IAN BRADY
H. CATHY WOOD
I. ANNIE WALTERS
J. GARY RICHARDS
K. DAVID BIRNIE
L. JOHN FISHER
M. ADOLFO CONSTANZO
N. NORMA BELL
O. RAYMOND FERNANDEZ

CONNECTING THE DOTS

More than one-fifth of all serial killers partner up with others to commit their crimes. Usually, the pairings involve one dominant person who exploits the insecurities, innocence, or mental instability of the other.

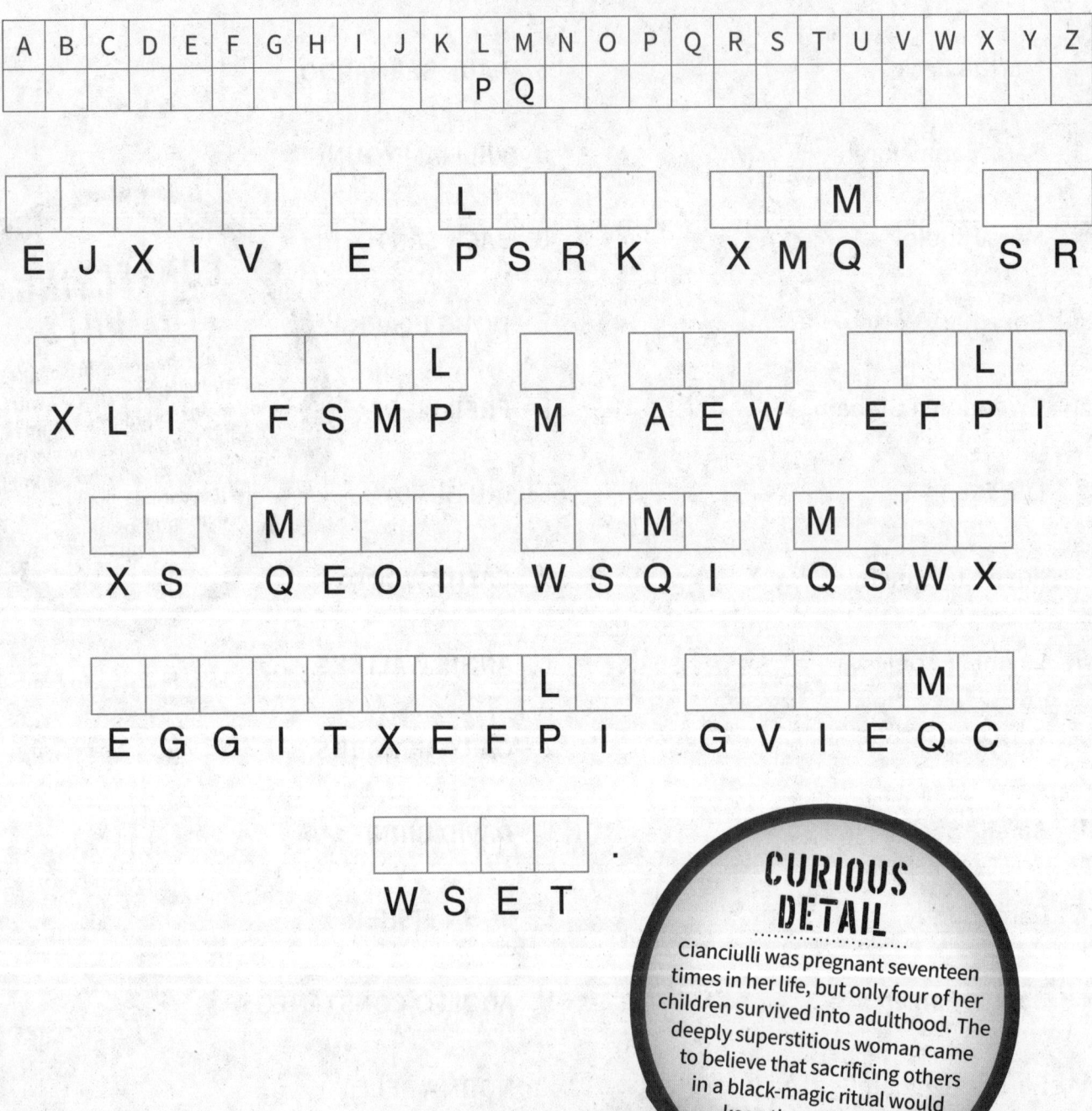

FEMME FATALES

KILLER RECALL

Test your true-crime knowledge with a quick chapter quiz.

1. Are female serial killers rarer or more abundant than their male counterparts?
   _____

2. Why did Dorothea Puente murder her tenants?
   _____

3. Which famous person did Susan Atkins murder?
   _____

4. Where did Betty Lou Beets bury her husband?
   _____

5. What did Leonarda Cianciulli make from her victims?
   _____

6. What condition resulted in Susan Smith killing her two sons?
   _____

7. Why do many women kill their partners and family members?
   _____

8. Which prolific serial killer was called "the Blood Countess"?
   _____

9. Who helped Paul Bernardo carry out several rapes and murders?
   _____

10. Waltraud Wagner led a group of nurses to kill how many patients?
    _____

ORGANIZED CRIMES

MOB BOSS MAYHEM

These figures headed up some of history's most notorious crime families and cartels.

ACROSS

4: A Chicago mob boss during Prohibition, he was infamous for bootlegging and tax evasion.
6: The leader of the Gambino crime family who's referred to as "the Teflon Don" and was known for evading convictions.
7: This financial mastermind behind organized crime operations was referred to as "the Mob's Accountant."
8: Leader of D-Company, this Indian crime boss was number three on the FBI's most-wanted list.
9: The Colombian drug lord who led the Medellín Cartel and controlled the global cocaine trade.

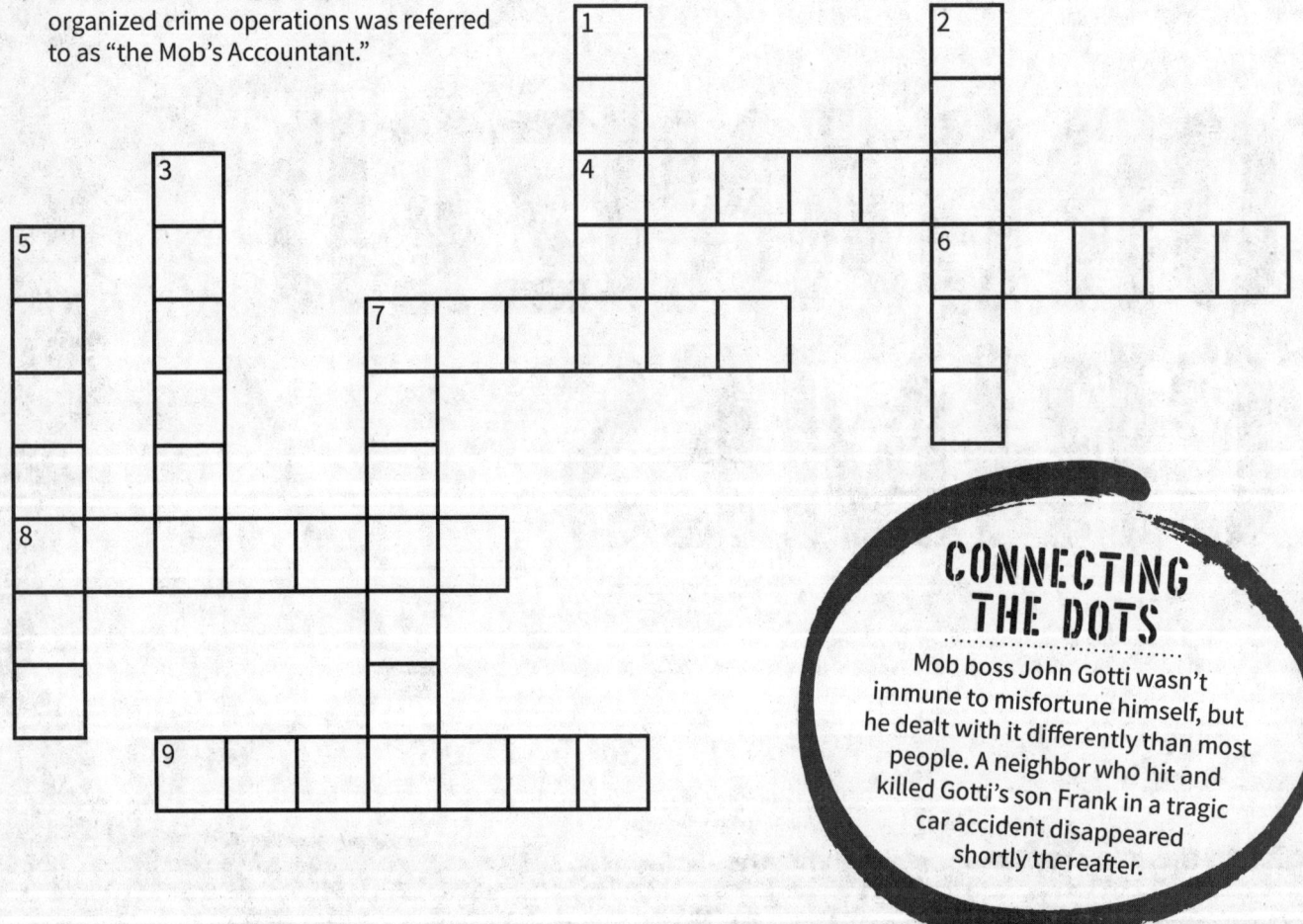

CONNECTING THE DOTS

Mob boss John Gotti wasn't immune to misfortune himself, but he dealt with it differently than most people. A neighbor who hit and killed Gotti's son Frank in a tragic car accident disappeared shortly thereafter.

DOWN

1: This Harlem drug kingpin smuggled heroin into the United States during the Vietnam War via military planes.
2: The notorious Las Vegas gangster who helped develop the city as a gambling mecca.
3: The Boston crime boss who led the Winter Hill Gang for years as an FBI informant.
5: This godfather of a prominent crime family was one of the most powerful Mafia leaders in history.
7: The Italian-American gangster credited with creating the modern Mafia structure in the United States.

ORGANIZED CRIMES

MAFIA MAP

Match these infamous criminals to the primary location of their illicit activities.

1. Al Capone
2. Bonnie and Clyde
3. Joaquín Guzmán
4. Yakuza
5. Camorra Crime Syndicate
6. Griselda Blanco
7. The Kray Twins
8. Salvatore Riina (Cosa Nostra)
9. Whitey Bulger
10. Semion Mogilevich
11. Charles "Lucky" Luciano
12. Frank Costello
13. Dawood Ibrahim
14. Pablo Escobar
15. Meyer Lansky

A. LAS VEGAS, NEVADA
B. MOSCOW, RUSSIA
C. TOKYO, JAPAN
D. SINALOA, MEXICO
E. MEDELLÍN, COLOMBIA
F. NEW YORK, NEW YORK
G. BOSTON, MASSACHUSETTS
H. SICILY, ITALY
I. MUMBAI, INDIA
J. SOUTHWESTERN USA
K. LONDON, ENGLAND
L. MIAMI, FLORIDA
M. NEW YORK, NEW YORK
N. NAPLES, ITALY
O. CHICAGO, ILLINOIS

CURIOUS DETAIL

At the height of his power, Pablo Escobar was one of the richest men in the world, with an estimated net worth of $30 billion—mostly from cocaine trafficking.

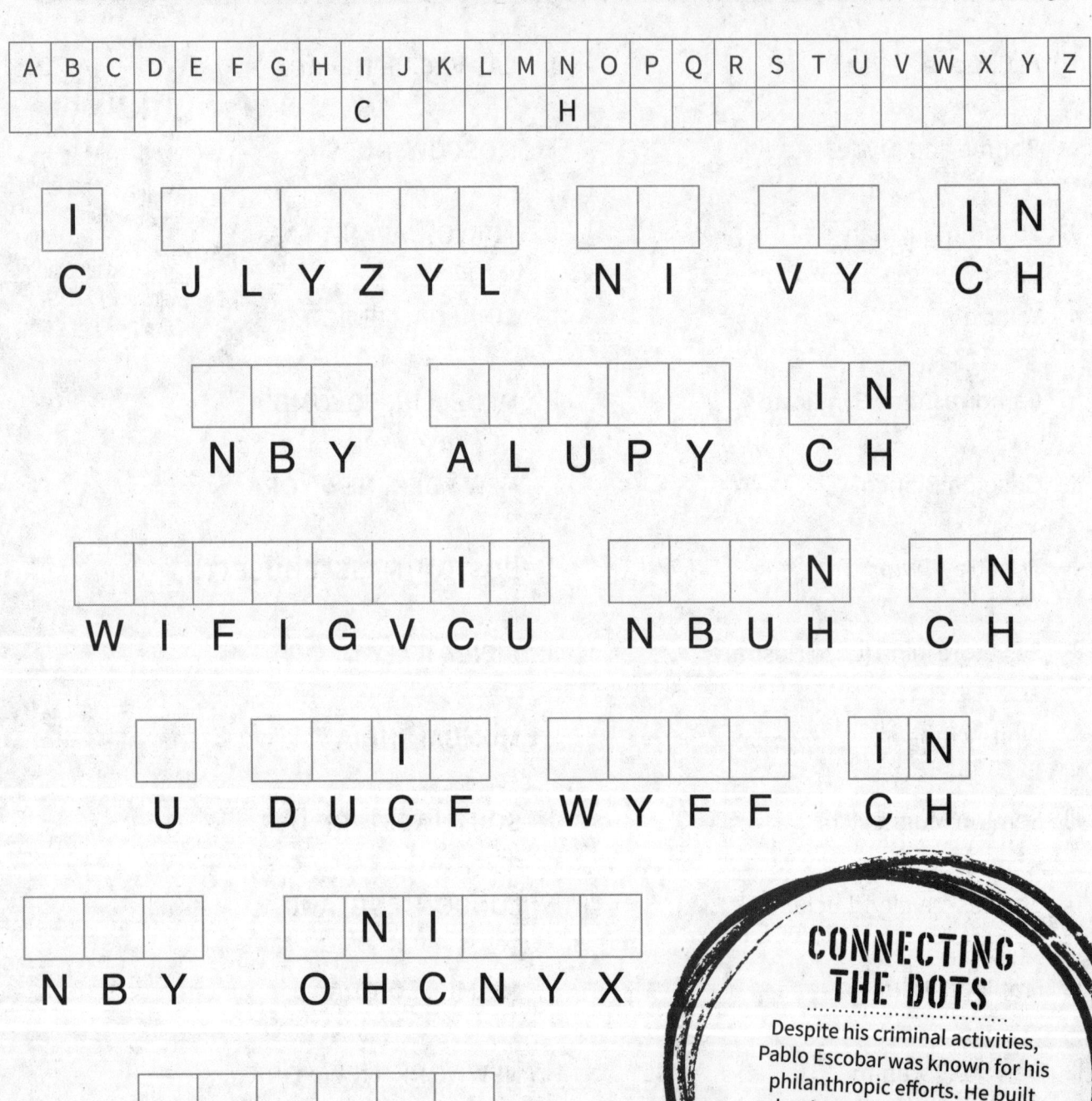

ORGANIZED CRIMES

UNDERWORLD ACTIVITIES

Expose all the activities that organized crime families are known for.

```
M G N I K C I F F A R T G U R D
N O I T P U R R O C B B A R G R
K D N N C F S Z Y L J S G N V P
I R D E R O X M A J S Y I N G G
D Y E A Y V N C U A T T L N Y B
N G U X Z L K S S G I X I L B R
A D N D T M A S P E G R J B G J
P B V I A O I U F I E L R D L L
P J R I N N R R N E R R I K L L
I K L I A N E T T D O A Z N K B
N D G T B T U E I B E Q C K G K
G Z I W N E K R B O N R L Y Z B
Q O N U Q C R E N Q N L I Y G Y
N D O K A B R Y P U V J W N M L
M C Z R N Y L L X K G Z X Z G N
```

Smuggling	Bribery	Kidnapping
Racketeering	Corruption	Fraud
Extortion	Assassination	Gunrunning
Money Laundering	Robbery	Blackmail
Drug Trafficking	Counterfeiting	Conspiracy

KILLER PUZZLES

ALIAS CHALLENGE

Decode the scrambled names of criminals based on their AKAs.

1. Known as "the Black Widow," she was infamous for her drug empire.

   DAEIRGLS ONLABC _____

2. Referred to as "the King of Cocaine," he was a major drug trafficker.

   LPOAB RSEBOCA _____

3. This notorious figure in the Genovese crime family was called "Chin."

   ETINVNC TGEGINA _____

4. Nicknamed "Joe Bananas," he was a leader known for his cunning strategies.

   OJE NBONAON _____

5. This head of the Sinaloa Cartel was known as "El Chapo."

   UQOJANÍ ZÁNMGU _____

6. The notorious underboss in the Gambino crime family who was referred to as "the Bull."

   MSAYM VNARAOG _____

7. Called "the Beast," he was a violent mobster and chief of the Sicilian Mafia.

   VREAALSOT IRIAN _____

ORGANIZED CRIMES

8. Appropriately nicknamed "the Iceman," this hitman froze his victims.

   HRCIRAD SKKNUIILK _____

9. He earned the nickname "Teflon Don" by dodging multiple convictions.

   NJHO TOTGI _____

10. Called "the Prime Minister" of the mob, this major American gangster was known for his influence in politics.

    KFANR LOLECSOT _____

11. Nicknamed "Skinny Joey," he was the reputed boss of a Philadelphia crime family until 2024.

    EJYO RIONMEL _____

12. This prominent figure in the Russian mob is known as "the Brainy Don."

    OSEIMN CILEOMHVICG _____

13. Referred to as "the General," he's one of the most well-known criminals in Irish history.

    TMIARN HCALIL _____

14. Famously nicknamed "Lucky," this mobster is considered the father of the Italian-American Mafia.

    SRAHCEL NOAIUCL _____

> **CURIOUS DETAIL**
> Al Capone got his nickname, "Scarface," not from his criminal exploits but from a scar he received during a fight in his youth. He wasn't a fan of the name, though, preferring "Big Al," which he felt was more approachable.

KILLER PUZZLES

GANGSTERS ONSCREEN

Discover these legendary gangster films and TV shows based on their descriptions.

ACROSS

3: Tony Montana's rise in Miami's drug trade showcases ambition's excesses and violent consequences.

4: (2 wds.) Denzel Washington stars as Frank Lucas, a heroin dealer in 1970s Harlem.

6: (2 wds.) Mob boss Tony Soprano balances crime and personal struggles.

8: The rise of drug kingpin Pablo Escobar and the DEA's efforts to take him down.

10: The true story of Henry Hill's rise in the mob and the thrills and dangers of organized crime.

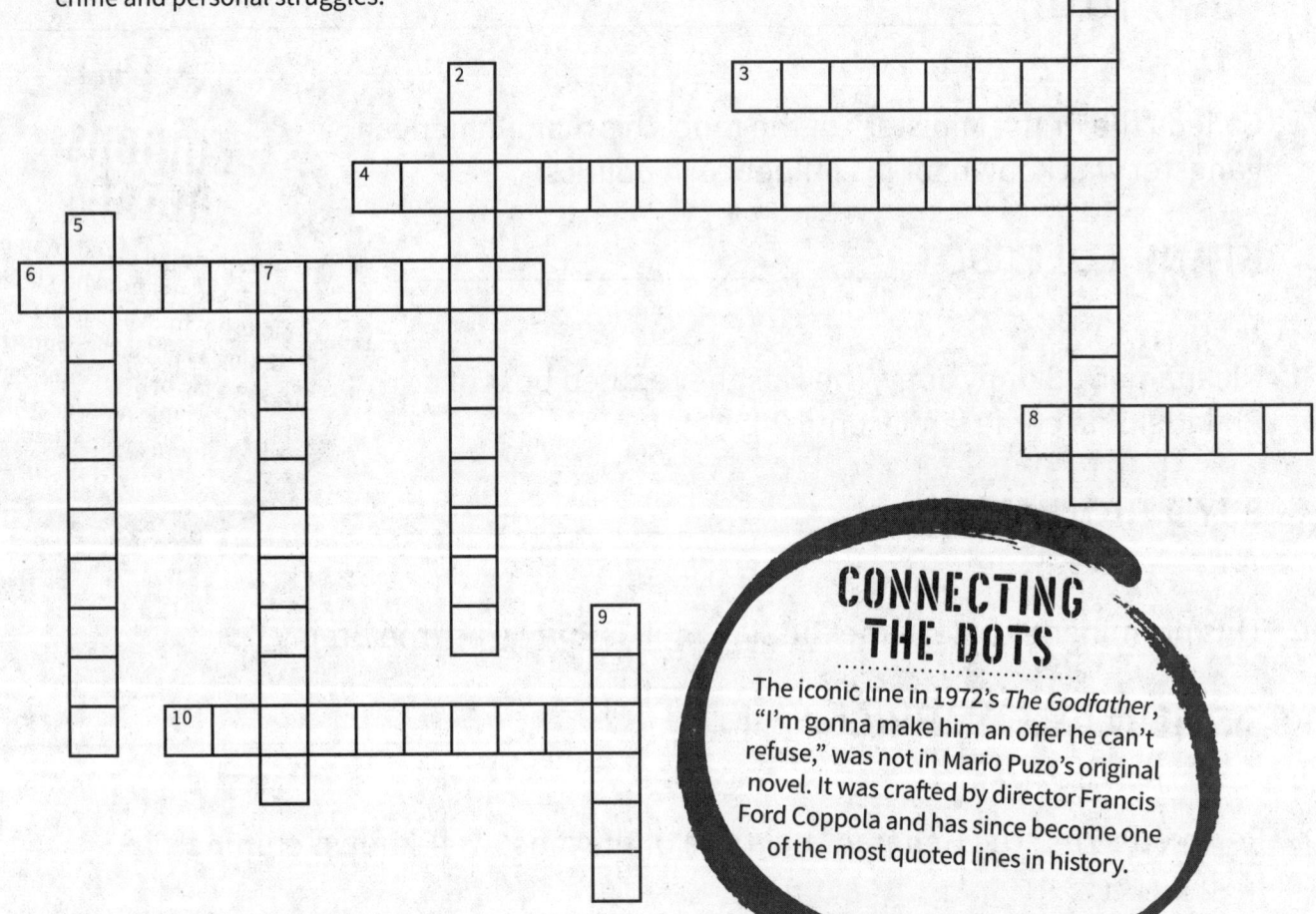

CONNECTING THE DOTS

The iconic line in 1972's *The Godfather*, "I'm gonna make him an offer he can't refuse," was not in Mario Puzo's original novel. It was crafted by director Francis Ford Coppola and has since become one of the most quoted lines in history.

DOWN

1: (2 wds.) Hitman Frank Sheeran reflects on his ties to the Bufalino crime family and his connection to Jimmy Hoffa.

2: (2 wds.) The Corleone crime family navigates loyalty and betrayal in postwar America.

5: (2 wds.) An undercover cop and a mole in the police force try to identify each other while infiltrating an Irish gang in Boston.

7: (2 wds.) Quentin Tarantino weaves together multiple stories involving hitmen, mobsters, and a mysterious briefcase.

9: The rise and fall of a Las Vegas executive with ties to the mob.

COPPOLA'S WARNING

Francis Ford Coppola's 1974 sequel *The Godfather Part II* includes this pivotal quote that perfectly encapsulates the dynamics of organized crime.

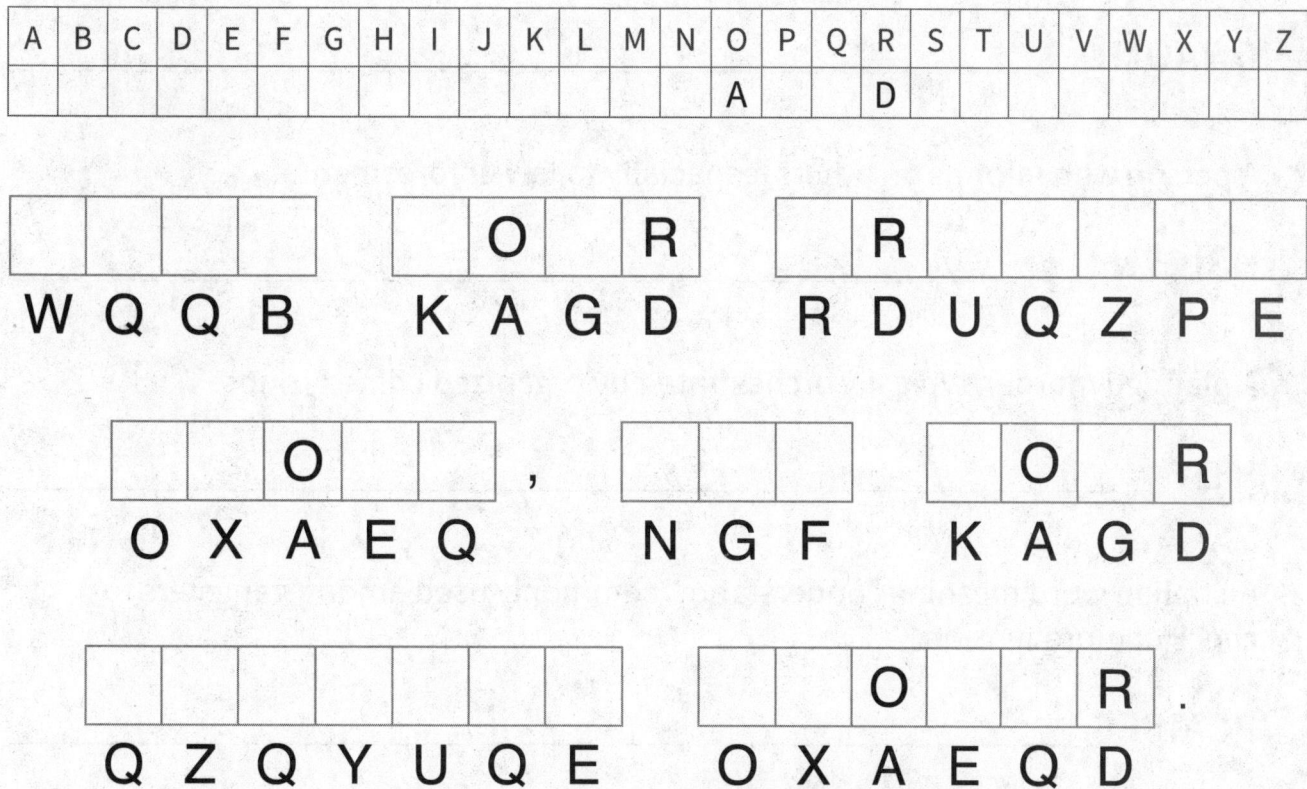

# GRITTY GLOSSARY

Unscramble the gangster lingo.

1. Slang for money, often used in the context of making or losing cash.

   OHAOML _____

2. A person who informs on others, especially to law enforcement.

   HSICTN _____

3. A planned murder, typically orchestrated by organized crime groups.

   HTI _____

4. An Italian word meaning "understand," commonly used among gangsters to check comprehension.

   PCAISEC _____

5. An old-fashioned slang term for a detective or private investigator.

   EOHSMGU _____

6. A hired thug or enforcer, often used to intimidate people or do the dirty work.

   ONGO _____

7. A member of a violent criminal organization, particularly associated with the Mafia.

   RMESTOB _____

ORGANIZED CRIMES

8. A person who has escaped from custody or is on the run from law enforcement.

   ITIFVGUE _____

9. Someone who is set up to take the blame for a crime.

   SPYAT _____

10. A slang term for a crime, often implying a daring or clever operation.

    PECRA _____

11. An informant who betrays their criminal associates to law enforcement.

    ATR _____

12. A makeshift knife or weapon, often used in prisons.

    VHIS _____

13. To snitch on someone; alternatively, a ten-year prison sentence.

    DEMI _____

14. The territory controlled and protected by a gang or criminal organization.

    FTRU _____

CONNECTING THE DOTS

Many Mafia terms have Italian roots, thanks in large part to the Five Families (the five major Italian-American Mafia families rooted in New York City circa 1931): Bonanno, Colombo, Gambino, Genovese, and Lucchese.

CAPONE'S DEFENSE

American gangster Al Capone's defense showcased the blurred lines between crime and commerce in the Prohibition era.

A	B	C	D	E	F	G	H	I	J	K	L	M	N	O	P	Q	R	S	T	U	V	W	X	Y	Z
												R								Y					

☐ ' **M** ☐ ☐ **T** ☐
N   R   S T Y   F

M ☐ ☐ **T** ☐ ☐ .
R   T S   X Y J W

CURIOUS DETAIL

Capone's assertion reflects his attempt to legitimize his image, which motivated him to fund charitable efforts, such as soup kitchens, during the Great Depression—while he was bootlegging and gambling.

☐ ' **M** ☐
N   R   F

☐ ☐ ☐ ☐ ☐ ☐ ☐ ☐ **M** ☐ .
G Z X N S J X X R F S

ORGANIZED CRIMES

CRACKING DOWN ON CRIME

Canvas the grid to find these law enforcement-related words.

```
N P A T E R I W N N L T R
E O R T N V T T Q G A G S
C P I R E V I T S S D D Z
N R C T E S J T K E I M T
A O O Y A V T F C A R N W
L S R Y R G O I R E A R B
L E R J T R I C M M T T A
I C U Q C N R T R O P E Q
E U P E F Y U O S E N T D
V T T Z B B F O R E D Y K
R I I D I N M I B D V N T
U O O N I T C Z V R Z N U
S N N Y R O N X B V Q L I
```

FBI	Arrest	Raids
RICO	Wiretap	Informant
Undercover	Prosecution	Corruption
Surveillance	Testimony	Detective
Investigation	Taskforce	Bounty

87

MOBSTER METHODS

Match each famous organized-crime figure to their crime of choice.

1. Carlos Marcello
2. Whitey Bulger
3. Vito Genovese
4. Jack McGurn
5. Nicky Barnes
6. Anthony Stabile
7. Paul Castellano
8. Joaquín Guzmán
9. Abe Reles
10. Salvatore Gravano
11. Frank Lucas
12. Lucky Luciano
13. Griselda Blanco
14. Anthony Salerno
15. Gennaro Catena

A. NATIONAL CRIME SYNDICATE
B. TESTIFYING AGAINST ASSOCIATES
C. DRUG TRAFFICKING
D. BOOTLEGGING
E. SMUGGLING HEROIN
F. UNION CORRUPTION
G. MURDERING RIVALS
H. CONSTRUCTION KICKBACKS
I. PROTECTION RACKET
J. RACKETEERING
K. HEROIN DISTRIBUTION
L. INFORMING
M. COCAINE TRAFFICKING
N. AIRPORT HIJACKINGS
O. PLANNING A MASSACRE

CONNECTING THE DOTS

James "Whitey" Bulger hated his nickname but loved prison. He once said, "If I could choose my epitaph on my tombstone, it would be 'I'd rather be in Alcatraz.'" Which is odd, considering his later career choice.

ORGANIZED CRIMES

KILLER RECALL

Test your true-crime knowledge with a quick chapter quiz.

1. What city is Bugsy Siegel credited for contributing to the development of?

2. Where did numbers guy Meyer Lansky commit his crimes?

3. True or false: Pablo Escobar had a complicated relationship with the public due to his philanthropic efforts, despite his criminal activity.

4. Which Colombian drug lord was referred to as "the Black Widow"?

5. True or false: Al Capone got his nickname "Scarface" from an altercation with other mobsters at the height of his power.

6. Which film was based on the crimes of Frank Lucas?

7. What was Lucky Luciano most well known for?

8. What did Al Capone call himself when defending his actions on trial?

9. What is the slang term for someone who informs on others?

10. What was the nickname for Joaquín Guzmán, leader of the Sinaloa Cartel?

CULT KILLINGS

KILLER PUZZLES

INFAMOUS CULT LEADERS

Identify these dangerous cult leaders based on their destructive legacies.

ACROSS

1: The polygamist leader who headed the Fundamentalist Church of Jesus Christ of Latter-Day Saints.
4: The leader of Heaven's Gate who convinced followers to "exit" to join a UFO.
7: This Japanese cult leader was behind the 1995 Tokyo subway sarin attack.
8: (2 wds.) The self-proclaimed messiah, who founded the Unification Church in Korea in 1954.
9: Claiming to be a Christlike messiah, he led the religious sect targeted in the Waco siege of 1993.

CONNECTING THE DOTS

The Branch Davidians didn't die out after the deadly FBI raid of their Waco compound. Some who survived rebuilt with a new name ("Branch, The Lord Our Righteousness") and a new leader (Charles Pace).

DOWN

1: As the founder of the Peoples Temple, he was responsible for the 1978 mass suicide in Jonestown.
2: (2 wds.) He led a religious commune called the Source Family, which centered around New Age philosophies in the 1970s.
3: The family convicted for orchestrating multiple brutal murders in California in 1969.
5: This criminal led the Children of God, which promoted a doctrine of "Flirty Fishing."
6: He founded NXIVM, which abused women and branded them with his initials.

MASTERS OF INFLUENCE

Match each cult with its ambitious leader.

1. Heaven's Gate
2. The Manson Family
3. Branch Davidians
4. The Peoples Temple
5. The Order of the Solar Temple
6. Scientology
7. The Family
8. Children of God
9. NXIVM
10. Aum Shinrikyo
11. Rajneesh Movement
12. The Process Church of the Final Judgment
13. The Church of the Firstborn of the Lamb of God
14. Love Has Won
15. Order of Nine Angles

A. DAVID BERG
B. MARY ANN MACLEAN AND ROBERT DE GRIMSTON
C. SHOKO ASAHARA
D. AMY CARLSON
E. MARSHALL APPLEWHITE
F. CHARLES MANSON
G. ANTON LONG
H. L. RON HUBBARD
I. KEITH RANIERE
J. ANNE HAMILTON-BYRNE
K. ERVIL LEBARON
L. JOSEPH DI MAMBRO AND LUC JOURET
M. DAVID KORESH
N. BHAGWAN SHREE RAJNEESH
O. JIM JONES

CURIOUS DETAIL

The Order of Nine Angles claims to have been founded in the 1960s by a nameless woman, and its current leader goes by a pseudonym. Authorities believe his real identity to be that of British neo-Nazi David Myatt, though he's denied involvement.

KILLER PUZZLES

JONES'S MANIPULATION

This chilling quote from Jim Jones came from an audio recording he made just before the mass suicide in Jonestown, where he manipulated his victims into believing they were part of a noble cause.

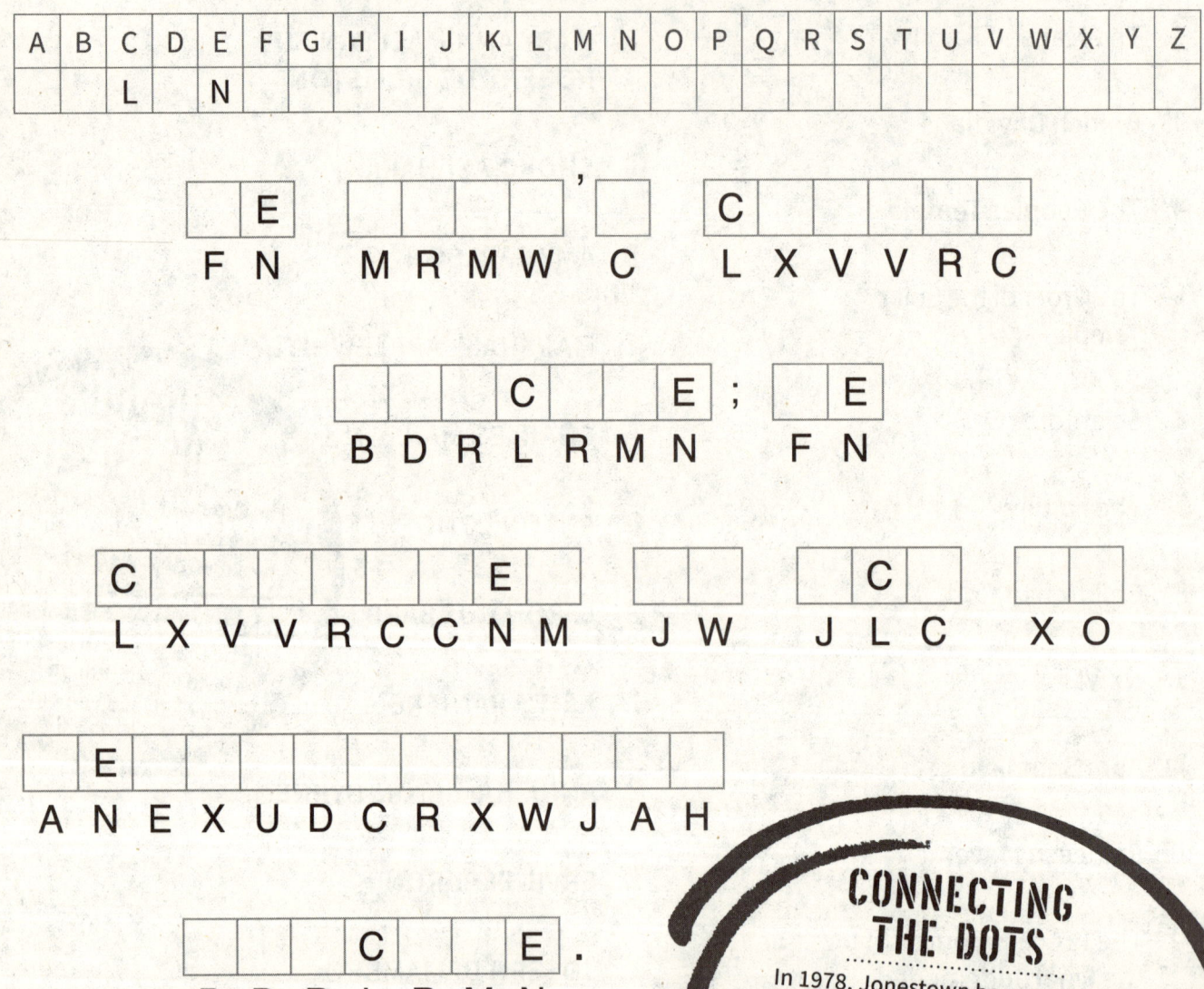

CONNECTING THE DOTS

In 1978, Jonestown became the site of the largest mass suicide in modern history, where over 900 cult followers died. But not all of them went willingly. Those who didn't drink the cyanide-laced punch were with injected with the poison. This is where the phrase "drinking the Kool-Aid" comes from, although they technically used Flavor Aid.

SEARCH FOR SECRETS

Expose the tactics and rituals often used within cults.

```
I B S H I E R A R C H Y
N T N Y Q Y P A E K R N
I E M X M X C R M I M L
T G T E J B E E T G P L
I A C L D M O U R R O N
A M Z H O I A L O C A D
T I S N A L T P I M E S
I R Y I I N H A S S A S
O G H S G E T I T C M P
N L T T C I L I R I Y V
T I N Y A A L E N T O B
C P L W T O D M D G V N
```

Initiation	Meditation	Chanting
Ceremony	Sigil	Talisman
Symbolism	Sacred	Ritualistic
Hierarchy	Dogma	Secrecy
Oath	Prophecy	Pilgrimage

DARK DESTINATIONS

Unscramble the words to reveal the locations of notorious cult tragedies.

1. The city where the Heaven's Gate cult members committed mass suicide, believing they would ascend to a spaceship trailing the Hale-Bopp comet in 1997.

   OCARNH TNSAE EF _____

2. The city where the Order of the Solar Temple cult carried out murders in 1994.

   CEQBEU _____

3. The city where the Manson Family cult carried out the brutal murder of actress Sharon Tate in 1969.

   OLS SENAGLE _____

4. The state where David Berg's Children of God cult was involved in notorious child exploitation scandals.

   ACARILNFO _____

5. The capital city where the leader of the Shining Path, a Maoist guerrilla cult, orchestrated violent campaigns in the 1980s and early 1990s.

   MIAL _____

6. The state where Bhagwan Shree Rajneesh's cult attempted to poison local residents during a biological attack in 1984.

   NORGEO _____

7. The city where the Shincheonji Church of Jesus cult was involved in a massive COVID-19 outbreak and accused of purposely spreading the virus.

   UDEAG _____

CULT KILLINGS

8. The capital city where Aum Shinrikyo cult members released sarin gas in a subway, leading to multiple deaths in 1995.

   OYOKT _____

9. The country where the Holy Spirit Movement cult, led by Alice Lakwena, was involved in a violent rebellion against the government in the 1980s.

   GAAUND _____

10. The Australian state where The Family, led by Anne Hamilton-Byrne, performed brainwashing experiments on children in the 1960s and 70s.

    IARTVOCI _____

11. The remote country where a violent doomsday cult, led by Jim Jones, conducted horrific rituals and forced druggings in the 1970s.

    NAYGAU _____

12. The country where the Brethren cult members faced criminal charges for ritualistic practices that led to multiple deaths in the 1990s.

    AILRBZ _____

13. The region where the Church of the Last Testament died by suicide or for lack of medical care in the 1990s.

    IRSBIAE _____

14. The state where a radical offshoot of the Church of Scientology was accused of abuse and harassment in the 1970s.

    IICLANROAF _____

> **CURIOUS DETAIL**
>
> Members of the Order of the Solar Temple believed they would be reborn on a distant planet. After facing increasing scrutiny for illegal arms trafficking, their leader claimed that the stars were aligned for his followers' final act of devotion—a chilling mass suicide.

CULT CLASSICS

Which movie titles adorn these cult-centric stories?

ACROSS

7: (2 wds.) A man attends a dinner party hosted by his ex-wife and her new husband and gradually uncovers their cultlike beliefs.

8: A French horror series that features a supernatural cult.

9: Friends travel to Sweden for a festival and find themselves caught in the rituals of a pagan cult.

10: (2 wds.) Two brothers return to the cult they escaped from and face strange occurrences.

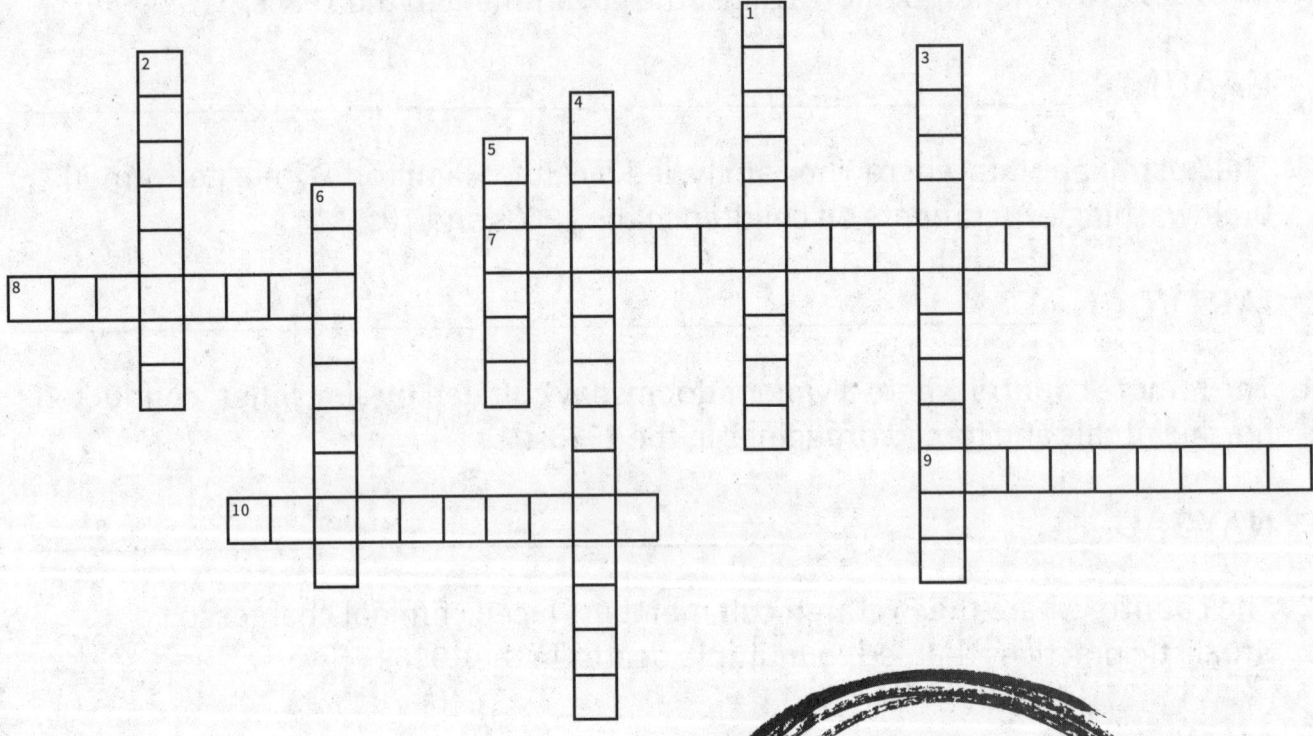

DOWN

1: After the death of their matriarch, a grieving family discovers a secret cult with dark intentions.

2: (2 wds.) A hitman connects with a cult while carrying out a series of assassinations.

3: (3 wds.) A policeman investigates a missing child on a remote Scottish island and discovers a disturbing cult.

4: (2 wds.) A pregnant woman suspects that an occult group wants to take her baby.

5: (2 wds.) A young Black man discovers the sinister practices of his white girlfriend's family.

6: (2 wds.) A World War II veteran becomes involved with a charismatic leader and his movement.

CONNECTING THE DOTS

A psychoanalyst and psychology professor at Tufts University, Dr. Stanley H. Cath, noticed an interesting trend among cult members: many of them had rejected mainstream religion before going all-in on religious cults.

KORESH'S CONCEIT

Branch Davidian David Koresh made it clear in this quote that being a cult leader has a lot to do with thinking you are God.

CURIOUS DETAIL

Before assuming leadership of the Branch Davidians, Koresh was a musician. He often wrote and performed songs that conveyed his interpretations of biblical prophecies. His music was a tool to attract followers, showcasing his charisma and ability to connect with his congregation.

FATAL PROPHECIES

Unscramble the names of doomsday cults based on the apocalyptic events they predicted.

1. The cult that believed Earth would be "recycled" and committed suicide in 1997.

   SVAEEN'H TEGA _____

2. This group believed an apocalypse would occur in 1993 but died in a deadly standoff with authorities.

   NARCBH VIIADDNS _____

3. This Japanese cult predicted a world-ending conflict and carried out a deadly sarin gas attack on the subway in 1995.

   MUA OIYKRNISH _____

4. Believing they would face a nuclear apocalypse, this cult opted out with mass cyanide poisoning in 1978.

   OEEPLPS EEMTLP _____

5. Fearing apocalypse was imminent in the 1990s, members participated in mass suicides in Switzerland and Canada.

   LRAOS PTEMEL _____

6. This Siberian cult believes in a looming apocalypse and lives in seclusion while awaiting a new era.

   HRUCCH FO HET SATL AETMTTNES _____

CONNECTING THE DOTS

Many cults that predict doomsday often set specific dates for the apocalypse. When these dates pass without incident, the cognitive dissonance actually leads some followers to intensify their beliefs.

CULT KILLINGS

7. This UFO religion is preparing for an imminent alien return and the end of the world.

   ELIANRA NTMVEOEM _____

8. This cult predicted the end times in the 1970s, leading to the exploitation of children.

   ERDCLNIH FO DGO _____

9. This Australian cult prepared for the apocalypse by raising children in isolation.

   HET LYMAFI _____

10. This group believed in an apocalyptic race war they called "Helter Skelter."

    OSANMN YMAFIL _____

11. This doomsday cult believed in a catastrophic apocalypse in 1985, resulting in violence against nonbelievers.

    HTE ELBIB KASPES _____

12. This Texas-based cult predicted the end of the world multiple times, focusing on nuclear war and global destruction.

    SUOHE FO YHWEHA _____

13. This Christian sect gained attention in the 1970s and predicted that the world would end in 1981.

    WEN LAIELANC _____

14. Founded by Sun Myung Moon, this group believed in an impending apocalypse that would precede a new world order.

    NCTAOIUNIFI HCURHC _____

MANSON'S DEFLECTION

This Charles Manson quote encapsulates how he rationalized his family's murderous ways—by pointing the finger at society itself.

CURIOUS DETAIL

White supremacist Charles Manson believed that by committing a high-profile murder, like that of Sharon Tate, he could instigate social chaos and provoke a violent backlash against African Americans.

MIND GAMES

These mind control techniques are used by cults to attract and maintain followers.

```
N M A N I P U L A T I O N B W B
N O I T A V I R P E D P E E L S
D N I B R A I N W A S H I N G V
T D B T B Z Y N V Y C K D X R T
I N D G A D Y J V O N R X B Y G
S T E V C Z J R N I A P Z T W J
O T Z M K O I F H W V B N Q L N
L L R N H T E T E Z R A Y O J T
A R P U U S P R I Y M M R N Z P
T K K A S U I L C S J T L B T J
I Q L I O T L N I I N D Q M X T
O J O R Q L J R U O O E F E A R
N N G P X Q A Q C P W N S T R L
S L B Y P H R V N X Z N L E G D
Y D G D C P N D W R Y T M Y D L
```

Confessions	Groupthink	Manipulation
Brainwashing	Trust	Reward
Coercion	Sleep Deprivation	Desensitization
Ritual	Fear	Charisma
Isolation	Control	Punishment

SURVIVOR STORIES

Match the well-known figures with the cults they famously escaped from.

1. Janja Lalich
2. Bill Cosby
3. Bethany Joy Lenz
4. Joaquin Phoenix
5. Winona Ryder
6. Patricia Arquette
7. Sarah Edmondson
8. Megan Phelps-Roper
9. Michelle Pfeiffer
10. Toni Braxton
11. Glenn Close
12. Keira Maguire
13. Cheryl Rainfield
14. Leah Remini
15. Laura Johnston Kohl

A. THE SEASIDE SECT
B. PEOPLES TEMPLE
C. RAINBOW COMMUNE
D. BREATHARIANISM
E. SCIENTOLOGY
F. MOONIES
G. NXIVM
H. PILLAR OF TRUTH
I. WESTBORO BAPTIST CHURCH
J. DEMOCRATIC WORKERS PARTY
K. MORAL RE-ARMAMENT
L. CHILDREN OF GOD
M. THE BIG HOUSE FAMILY
N. KKK
O. SKYMONT SUBUD

CONNECTING THE DOTS

Research indicates that approximately 61.4 percent of men and 71.3 percent of women who leave cults struggle with PTSD. That's in stark contrast to the average rate of PTSD for Americans, which is 6.8 percent.

KILLER RECALL

Test your true-crime knowledge with a quick chapter quiz.

1. Which cult leader claimed to be a Christlike figure?
   _____

2. Which country was the site of the mass suicide that spawned the phrase "drinking the Kool-Aid?"
   _____

3. True or false: The Raelian Movement believes in aliens.
   _____

4. In what year did the Solar Temple enact mass murder-suicide?
   _____

5. Which horror film touches on the real practice of human sacrifice in Scotland?
   _____

6. What was David Koresh's occupation before assuming leadership of the Branch Davidians?
   _____

7. Which acclaimed actor from *The Joker* left the cult Children of God?
   _____

8. True or false: The rate of women who escape cults and experience PTSD as a result is higher than that of men.
   _____

9. What was the name of the cult that believed the Earth would be "recycled" in 1997?
   _____

10. Which Hollywood actress did the Manson Family target in 1969?
    _____

CULT KILLINGS

THE DARK SIDE OF FAME

KILLER PUZZLES

MUSICIANS' TRAGIC ENDS

Fill in the famous entertainers whose untimely deaths shocked the world.

ACROSS

3: A jazz bass virtuoso, he was beaten to death outside a nightclub in 1987.
7: This iconic rapper was fatally shot in a 1996 Las Vegas drive-by.
8: The legendary soul singer was killed by his father in a domestic dispute in 1984.
9: This rapper was shot in a robbery outside a motorcycle dealership in 2018.

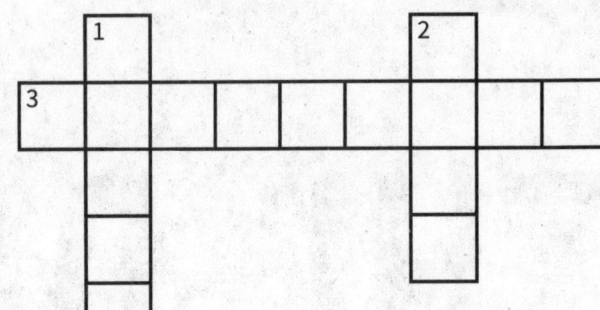
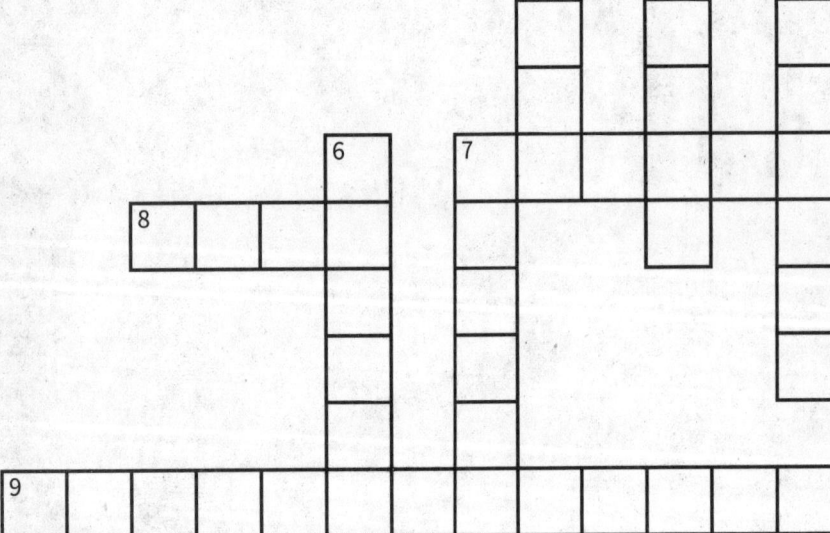

CONNECTING THE DOTS

Mark David Chapman was carrying a copy of *The Catcher in the Rye* at the time of his crime. He claimed that the novel influenced him to protect the world from his victim's "phoniness," puzzling the public.

DOWN

1: (3 wds.) This DJ of the pioneering rap group Run-D.M.C. was murdered in his Queens recording studio in 2002.
2: A member of the Bee Gees, he was shot during a dispute with a stalker in 2003.
4: The Jamaican reggae legend was killed in a violent home invasion in 1987.
5: A soul music icon, he was shot in a motel under mysterious circumstances in 1964.
6: The Beatles legend was shot outside his New York apartment building in 1980.
7: This beloved Tejano singer was shot by her fan club president in 1995.

THE DARK SIDE OF FAME

GONE TOO SOON

Match each celebrity to the year they met their tragic end.

1. The Notorious B.I.G.   A. 2004

2. Gianni Versace   B. 1962

3. Nicole Brown Simpson   C. 1993

4. Sharon Tate   D. 1997

5. Phil Hartman   E. 2016

6. Rebecca Schaeffer   F. 1994

7. Christina Grimmie   G. 1998

8. Bonny Lee Bakley   H. 2001

9. Adrienne Shelly   I. 2010

10. Lana Clarkson   J. 2006

11. Ronni Chasen   K. 1997

12. Dimebag Darrell   L. 1969

13. Mia Zapata   M. 1999

14. Marilyn Monroe   N. 1989

15. Jill Dando   O. 2003

CURIOUS DETAIL

Marilyn Monroe's death led to widespread conspiracy theories. But Monroe suffered from a variety of mental health disorders as well as endometriosis and gall bladder disease, according to experts, making her overdose heartbreaking but not exactly suspicious.

KILLER PUZZLES

CHANEL'S REMORSE

Fashion icon Coco Chanel is best remembered for the little black dress and her famous Chanel N°5 perfume, but this quote may have hinted at regret over her more covert legacy.

A	B	C	D	E	F	G	H	I	J	K	L	M	N	O	P	Q	R	S	T	U	V	W	X	Y	Z
								T							A										

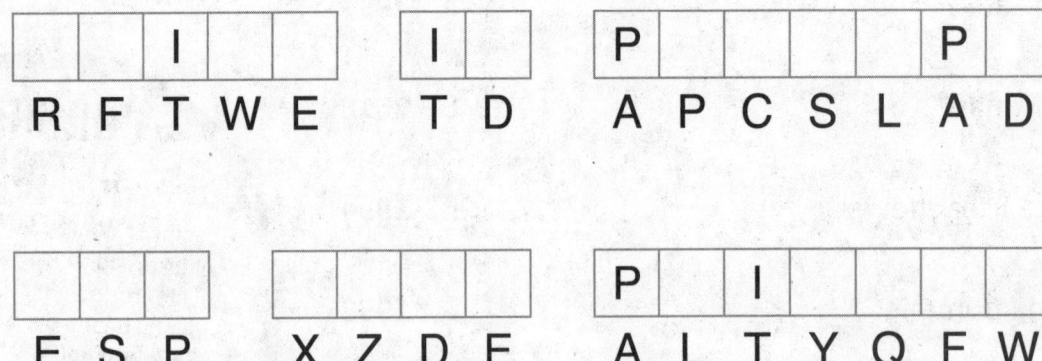

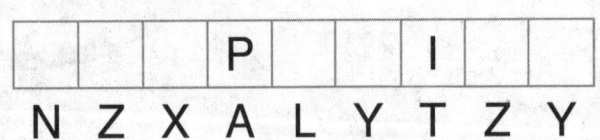

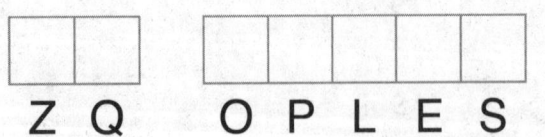

CONNECTING THE DOTS

During World War II, the French government arrested Chanel for alleged ties to Nazi intelligence. A lack of evidence (or, some say, strings pulled by Winston Churchill) saw her released, but she was, in fact, a collaborator.

THE DARK SIDE OF FAME

CIRCUMSTANCES OF DEATH

Search for the terms hidden in the grid associated with the circumstances of celebrity deaths.

```
A G A N G V I O L E N C E N Z
E S M G N N Y O H R Q T O V M
X Y S J N W I S V D E I M T P
E G Y A Z I A N R E T D L X Y
C B N R S R K O O A R U R P R
U T Z I C S W C L S A D V U G
T Y N R T N I U A S I D O N M
I G A E I O G N S J D O N S T
O C N N D N O A A U R T P B E
N J G I A I V H Y T I A W W B
M K Y R B T C R S L I C C Y J
R P T B D B G C B R M O I J Q
Y S V Z V J A N A D M Q N D Z
D J M W W R G T M D J R J L E
T T J Y J Z Z J S M Q X J R Z
```

Accident	Poisoning	Gang Violence
Murder	Car Crash	Execution
Overdose	Shooting	Carjacking
Assassination	Stabbing	Strangulation
Suicide	Drowning	Assault

KILLER PUZZLES

ATHLETES IN THE HOT SEAT

Unscramble the names of the players who got on the wrong side of the law.

1. The former NFL player accused and acquitted of the murders of Nicole Brown Simpson and Ron Goldman.

    J.O. MSNPISO _____

2. A former NFL player convicted of the 2013 murder of Odin Lloyd.

    RAANO HNDNAEREZ _____

3. The Paralympic athlete convicted of the 2013 shooting of his girlfriend Reeva Steenkamp.

    CSARO PSIRTOIUS _____

4. This NFL player was involved in a 2000 murder case, later pleading guilty to obstruction of justice.

    ARY WELIS _____

5. The boxer who was convicted of rape in 1992 and served three years in prison.

    EKMI YTSNO _____

6. This NBA star was accused of sexual assault in 2003, though the case was later settled out of court.

    EBOK NRYBAT _____

7. A former NFL player convicted in 2001 for conspiracy to murder his pregnant girlfriend, Cherica Adams.

    AER UTRHRAC _____

CURIOUS DETAIL

NFL players face a much higher rate of arrest for domestic violence than the average man, but they aren't the only athletes engaging in it. Floyd Mayweather continued to box until 2017 despite being convicted for domestic battery and assault five separate times.

THE DARK SIDE OF FAME

8. A figure skater involved in the 1994 attack on her rival that was orchestrated by her ex-husband.

   YATNO GNAIRHD _____

9. The NFL quarterback convicted in 2007 for his involvement in a dogfighting ring.

   LMACHIE CVKI _____

10. The NFL player who accidentally shot himself in the leg in 2008.

    LPAIXOC USSERBR _____

11. The NFL quarterback accused of sexual assault in 2009 and 2010.

    NEB REOTHGLSBERIER _____

12. An NFL player convicted of reckless assault in 2014 for disciplining his son with a switch.

    RDINAA PETRSONE _____

13. A US soccer star arrested multiple times for incidents that include domestic violence and disorderly conduct.

    EPOH OLSO _____

14. This Olympic sprinter was convicted in 2008 of lying to federal investigators about steroid use and involvement in check fraud.

    MOARIN SJOEN _____

15. The former NBA player convicted of voluntary manslaughter in connection with a 2011 shooting.

    VAJIRAS TOIRNETTNC _____

KILLER PUZZLES

HOLLYWOOD HEISTS

Use the clues like a map to the stars targeted by criminals.

ACROSS

5: This pop singer's home was robbed multiple times; among other valuables, burglars stole her 2014 Maserati.

7: The victim of a kidnapping plot in 2005, when his infant son was targeted by his house painter.

8: This judge's home was broken into in 2015 while he and his family were asleep inside.

10: The pop star and makeup mogul whose Los Angeles home was burglarized multiple times.

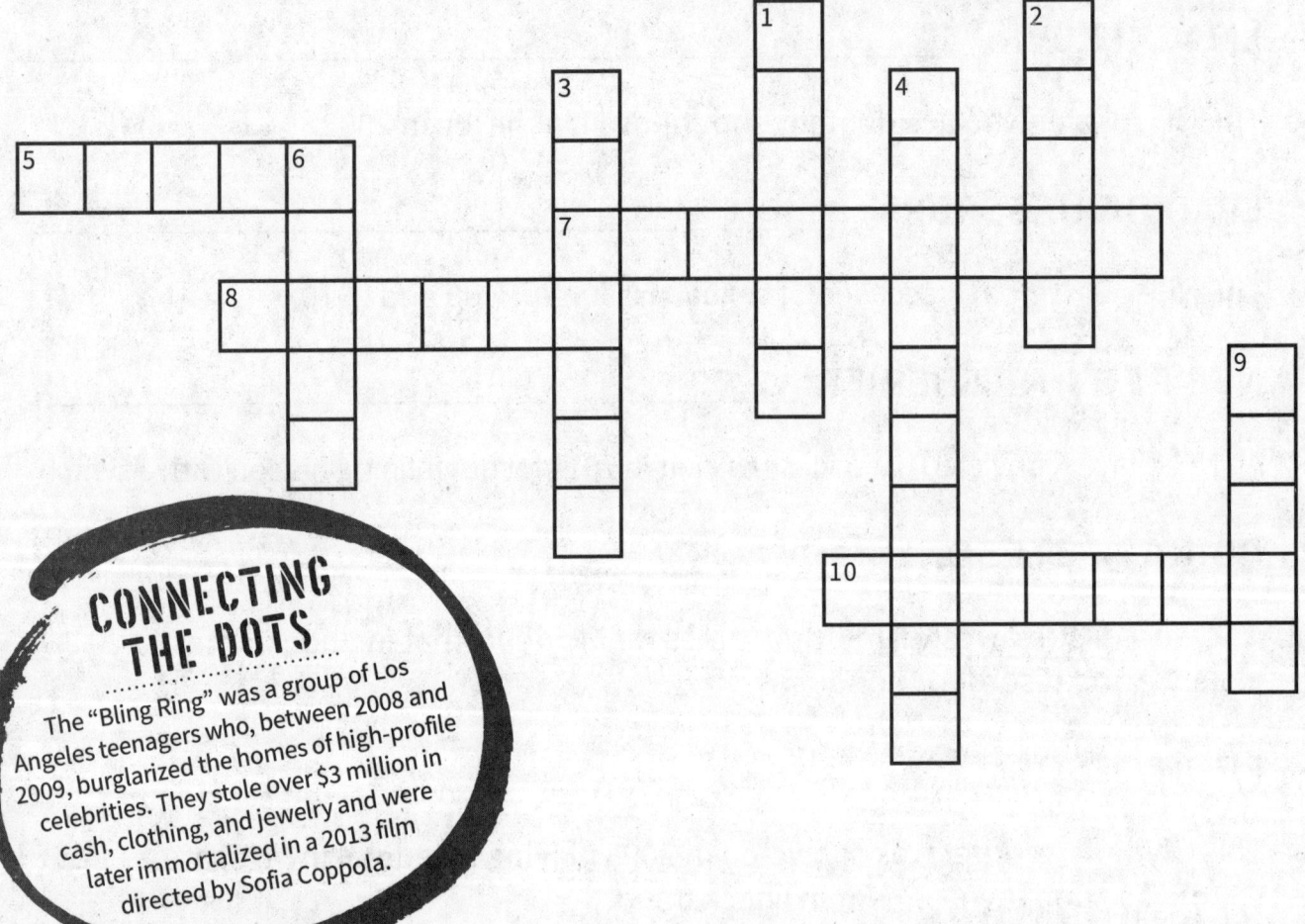

CONNECTING THE DOTS

The "Bling Ring" was a group of Los Angeles teenagers who, between 2008 and 2009, burglarized the homes of high-profile celebrities. They stole over $3 million in cash, clothing, and jewelry and were later immortalized in a 2013 film directed by Sofia Coppola.

DOWN

1: A victim of the Bling Ring burglaries, thieves stole the heiress's jewelry and clothing from her home.

2: The rapper lost $175,000 in jewelry and valuables when her Los Angeles home was burglarized near the end of 2016.

3: This *Speed* star was the victim of stalking and a home invasion in 2014.

4: She was robbed at gunpoint in Paris in 2016, losing millions in jewelry.

6: This *Basic Instinct* star was the victim of a home burglary in 2011.

9: Teens stole items from this redheaded actress's home in 2009 during the Bling Ring burglaries.

THE DARK SIDE OF FAME

SIMPSON'S SPECULATION

From his trial to his book, *If I Did It*, O. J. Simpson kept the public guessing about his innocence or guilt. This line from his 1998 interview with *Esquire* is a perfect example.

A	B	C	D	E	F	G	H	I	J	K	L	M	N	O	P	Q	R	S	T	U	V	W	X	Y	Z
			P	Q																					

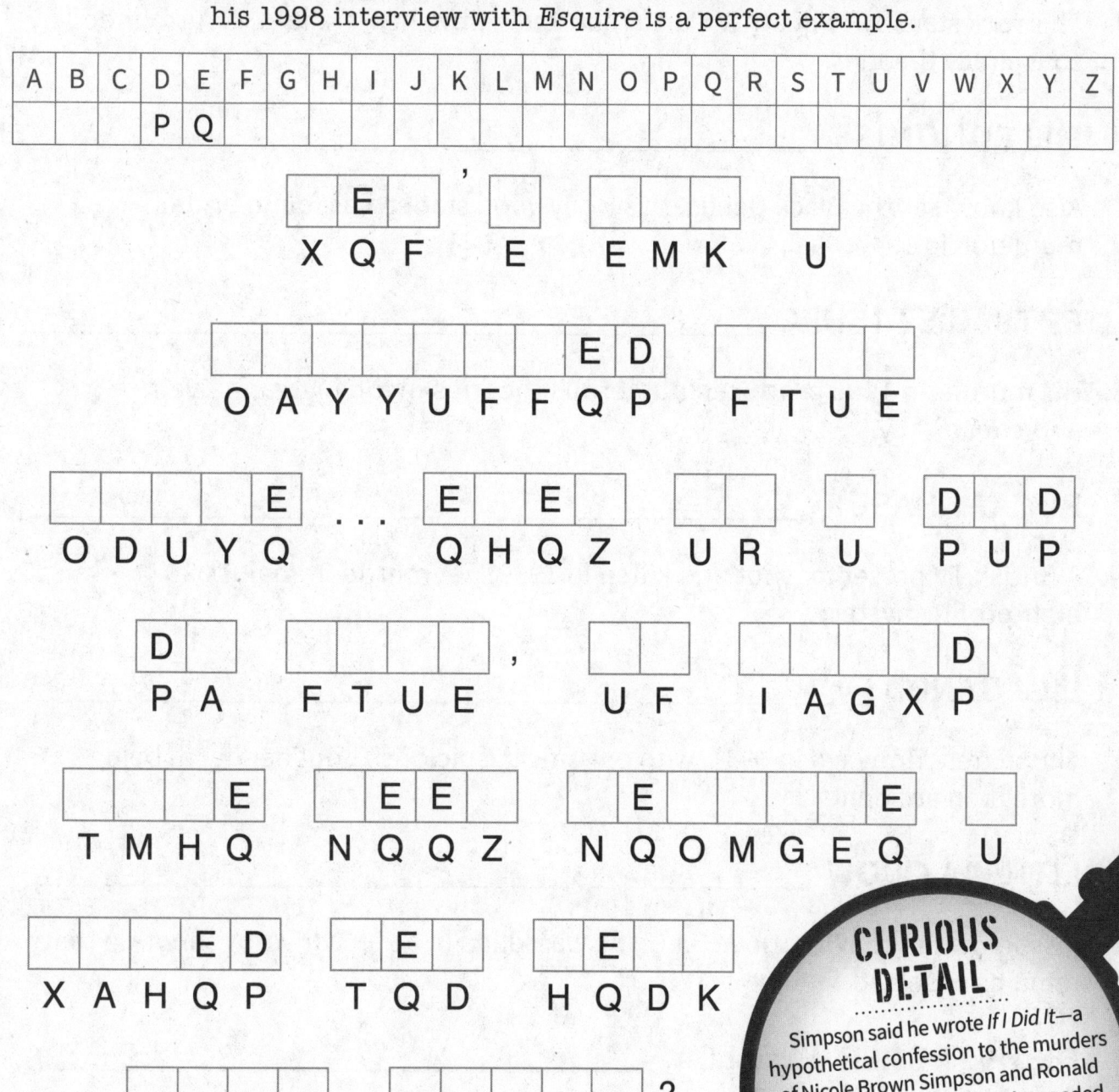

CURIOUS DETAIL

Simpson said he wrote *If I Did It*—a hypothetical confession to the murders of Nicole Brown Simpson and Ronald Goldman—simply because he needed money. The book was canceled by HarperCollins before being published by the Goldman family with a new subtitle: "Confessions of a Killer."

FALLEN STARS

Unscramble the names of the people whose deaths made national headlines.

1. This rock star's 1971 death in Paris, reportedly from heart failure, is surrounded by conspiracy theories.

   MIJ RONOMISR _____

2. Also known as the Black Dahlia, this Hollywood starlet was found brutally murdered in 1947.

   EHTBAILEZ TSHRO _____

3. His murder in 1996 produced numerous theories involving gang rivalry and conspiracy.

   PUCAT KHASUR _____

4. A British TV presenter shot and killed in 1999, her murder remains a high-profile mystery.

   LILJ OANDD _____

5. This actress drowned in 1981, with ongoing suspicions about her death being more than accidental.

   LITNEAA ODOW _____

6. Also known as the Notorious B.I.G., he was killed in a 1997 drive-by shooting that remains unsolved.

   HISHCTROPER WLEALCA _____

7. This famous fashion designer was murdered in 1997 on the steps of his Miami Beach mansion by serial killer Andrew Cunanan.

   INNGAI ESAVRCE _____

THE DARK SIDE OF FAME

8. The star of *Poltergeist*, she died in 1982 at just twenty-two years old after being murdered by her ex-boyfriend.

   MOQIDNEUI ENNDU _____

9. A jazz legend, this singer and pianist was fatally stabbed in a New York hotel in 1972.

   ELE RGONAM _____

10. This actor and martial artist was accidentally shot and killed on the set of *The Crow* in 1993.

    NBRONAD ELE _____

11. A famed publicist, she was shot and killed while driving home from a movie premiere in 2010.

    NINOR HSCENA _____

12. The lead singer of Pantera, he was shot and killed onstage by a deranged fan during a concert in 2004.

    BIADEMG DLLRERA _____

13. A well-known actor from *Diff'rent Strokes*, he was killed in 1998 during a robbery attempt at his home.

    TDDO IDGRBSE _____

14. The lead singer of The Gits, she was brutally raped and murdered in Seattle in 1993.

    IAM TAPAZA _____

> **CONNECTING THE DOTS**
>
> Bruce Lee's son hasn't been the only person killed on set by a prop gun. In 2021, actor Alec Baldwin accidentally shot and killed cinematographer Halyna Hutchinson the set of *Rust*.

117

KILLER PUZZLES

JACKSON'S IMMORTAL WORDS

Michael Jackson had this to say on the topic of his legacy—musical and otherwise.

PROTECTION METHODS

Search for the things celebrities have used to protect themselves against criminals.

```
R C B T Z N D T J R G Z W T Q S
S E A M M V T B R Y G N N B S T
U B D M X P P Y P R G M Z A L X
R W D R E T W W N N T D L L J R
V M G T O R P N D M M G Y L M P
E Z Y A K G A E N I F K Q N D G
I V G D R B N S S O S Y N R M K
L M R A X M R I O U T G A P T Q
L R O X T K O R N I O U U R D S
A D G O Y E P R R I G H A I M D
N Y D L R T S U E Y A C E R S X
C T Z E E C C J D D K R A F J E
E Z D L C E I O M E C L T P A M
R T L O S O B N R M A A D S J S
Y U G Y G N Y S A W G M R N E L
B T R D Z S J S K P W L L D K R
```

Bodyguard	Gates	Dogs
Security	Cameras	Bulletproof Glass
Surveillance	Decoys	Safe House
Alarms	Restraining Order	Panic Room
Armored Car	Disguise	Trackers

KILLER PUZZLES

CINEMATIC CRIMINALS

Match these fascinating films and documentaries to the criminals they depict.

1. *Zodiac*
2. *Killer Inside*
3. *Making a Murderer*
4. *Mindhunter*
5. *Extremely Wicked, Shockingly Evil and Vile*
6. *The Act*
7. *Caniba*
8. *The Staircase*
9. *American Murder*
10. *Catch Me If You Can*
11. *All Good Things*
12. *Conversations with a Killer*
13. *Tiger King*
14. *The Trials of Gabriel Fernandez*
15. *The Night Stalker*

A. ROBERT DURST
B. CHRIS WATTS
C. TED BUNDY
D. ZODIAC KILLER
E. JOE EXOTIC
F. RICHARD RAMIREZ
G. STEVEN AVERY
H. GYPSY ROSE BLANCHARD
I. MICHAEL PETERSON
J. FRANK WILLIAM ABAGNALE, JR.
K. DAVID BERKOWITZ
L. JOHN WAYNE GACY
M. ISAURO AGUIRRE
N. AARON HERNANDEZ
O. ISSEI SAGAWA

CONNECTING THE DOTS

When John F. Kennedy was assassinated on November 22, 1963, his last words were "No, they sure can't." It was his response to First Lady of Texas Nellie Connally asking him, "Mr. President, they can't make you believe now that there are not some in Dallas who love you and appreciate you, can they?"

KILLER RECALL

Test your true-crime knowledge with a quick chapter quiz.

1. Which of his family members killed soul singer Marvin Gaye?

2. What did Michael Jackson die of?

3. In what year was Nicole Brown Simpson killed?

4. What was NFL player Michael Vick convicted of?

5. Which Baldwin brother has been involved in both a robbery and a gun death?

6. True or false: Coco Chanel collaborated with the Nazis during World War II.

7. What was the Black Dahlia's real name?

8. True or false: Miley Cyrus's home has been burglarized multiple times.

9. Which influential rapper was fatally shot in a drive-by shooting in Las Vegas in 1996?

10. What were President John F. Kennedy's last words?

HISTORY-MAKING CASES

KILLER PUZZLES

LEGENDARY LAWBREAKERS

Fill in the names (or aliases) of these famous felons based on their descriptions.

ACROSS

4: The notorious cannibal whose victims police found in pieces in his apartment.
7: Known for his cultlike following, he claimed he was guided by demons to murder.
8: (2 wds.) A serial killer active in California who left taunting letters; still unidentified.
10: The "Killer Clown" who set the stage for the FBI's behavioral science unit.

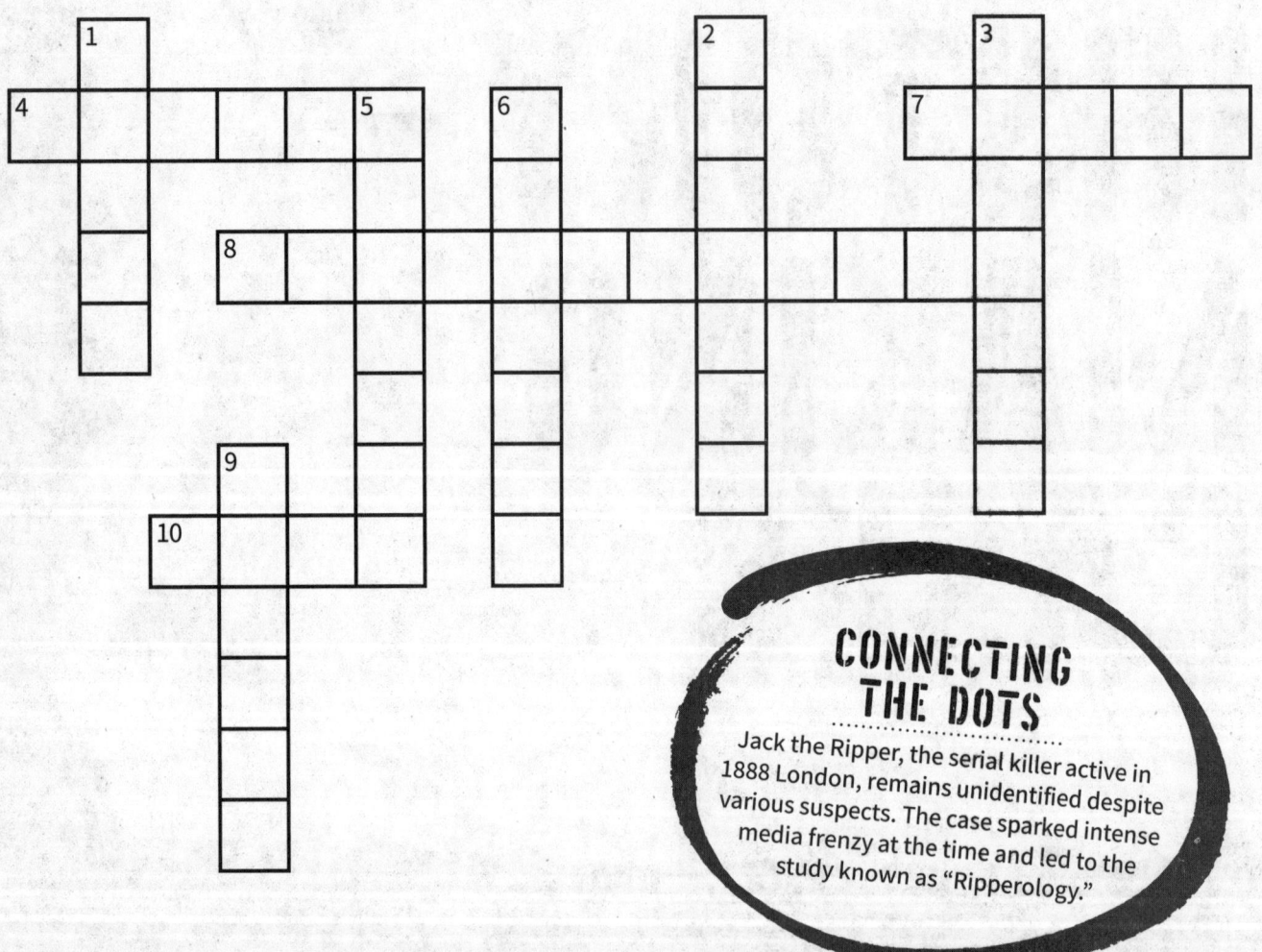

CONNECTING THE DOTS

Jack the Ripper, the serial killer active in 1888 London, remains unidentified despite various suspects. The case sparked intense media frenzy at the time and led to the study known as "Ripperology."

DOWN

1: The "BTK Killer" who eluded capture for decades.
2: The "Night Stalker" who killed children in the 1980s.
3: The female serial killer who was executed in Florida for killing seven men.
5: Known as the "Green River Killer," he confessed to murdering more than forty-nine women.
6: The 1980 assassin who was infamous for his "not guilty" plea by reason of insanity.
9: The cult leader who orchestrated a series of brutal murders in 1969.

CRIMINAL CONNECTIONS

Match the high-profile convict to the brief description of their infamous crime.

1. Rae Carruth
2. Mary Bell
3. Elizabeth Holmes
4. Jared Loughner
5. James Holmes
6. Ted Kaczynski
7. Derek Chauvin
8. Richard Speck
9. Harvey Weinstein
10. Chad Daybell
11. Karla Homolka
12. Al Capone
13. Aaron Hernandez
14. Amanda Knox
15. Robert Durst

A. SEXUAL ASSAULT AND ABUSE
B. MURDERED ROOMMATE
C. KILLED GEORGE FLOYD
D. SHOT GABBY GIFFORDS
E. KILLED WIFE AND CHILDREN
F. KILLED ODIN LLOYD
G. RAPE AND MURDER
H. MOVIE THEATER SHOOTING
I. CONSPIRED TO KILL GIRLFRIEND
J. KILLED EIGHT NURSES
K. STARTUP FRAUD
L. KILLED WIFE
M. UNABOMBER ATTACKS
N. KILLED TWO BOYS
O. BOOTLEGGING

CURIOUS DETAIL

Wealthy real estate heir Robert Durst became notorious for several mysterious disappearances, including that of his wife, Kathleen, in 1982. His story gained renewed attention with HBO's *The Jinx*, in which he was overheard saying, "What the hell did I do? Killed them all, of course."

MANSON'S MOTIVATION

Charles Manson loved to make a dramatic impact with his words as well as his murders, which is obvious from this quote.

A	B	C	D	E	F	G	H	I	J	K	L	M	N	O	P	Q	R	S	T	U	V	W	X	Y	Z
					E						L														

☐☐ ☐O☐'☐☐ ☐☐O☐☐☐
F C   V L R   O B   D L F K D

☐O ☐O☐ ☐O☐☐ ☐☐H☐☐,
Q L   A L   P L J B   Q E F K D

☐O☐☐☐.
A L   F Q T B I I

CONNECTING THE DOTS

Charles Manson was an aspiring musician who leveraged his connections to high-profile musicians like the Beach Boys. He even wrote part of their song "Never Learn Not to Love."

☐☐☐☐ ☐☐☐☐
X K A   I B X S B

☐O☐☐H☐☐ ☐☐☐☐H☐.
P L J B Q E F K D   T F Q Z E V

LEGAL JARGON

Uncover the terms related to legal tools and milestones.

```
T V R R Y P Y N R D J N N M L R
D E F E N S E T U M N N L P E T
T L D D S N V E I S Q I K S B Z
R I K O T T P S U L B M T D Z V
R B V G U R I B C I I R P M B T
K G M A O B P T L I A B Y B Z J
M S Y C D O L A U I S T A W B K
Y I E B E I Y E N T I N N I B M
L S R N Y P F I J N I A E D L T
S Y A A T J N F A E Y O E R Z L
N L Y M N G M S A B O T N L O L
D A P P O D N L A E P P A N P F
Q N R R Z I A K L B W Z A N W Q
Y A D Y M B Q T R L B R Y R X Q
D E Y L N K V V B M M T Y N D M
R N L M D Q N V M Y Z X N Z V Y
```

Miranda	Forensics	Affidavit
Analysis	Plea	Alibi
Insanity	Liability	Double Jeopardy
Defense	Restraining Order	Subpoena
Due Process	Restitution	Appeal

SITES OF INFAMY

Unscramble each location where these history-making murders occurred.

1. In 1947, Elizabeth Short's body was found mutilated and bisected here.

   OLS EESNGAL _____

2. Lee Harvey Oswald assassinated President John F. Kennedy in broad daylight in this city.

   LADLSA _____

3. In 1888, Jack the Ripper terrorized this capital city.

   OLNNOD _____

4. The 1929 St. Valentine's Day Massacre, ordered by Al Capone, stained this city with blood.

   HICGCAO _____

5. The city where James Earl Ray assassinated Dr. Martin Luther King, Jr. in 1968.

   PHMMESI _____

6. In this New Jersey city, Bruno Hauptmann kidnapped and murdered the Lindbergh baby in 1932.

   EHOPLWEL _____

7. Albert DeSalvo terrorized this city in the early 1960s by strangling thirteen women.

   SOBNOT _____

HISTORY—MAKING CASES

8. The "Zodiac Killer" murdered multiple victims in this area in the late 1960s.

   ASN RFNACCIOS _____

9. Aileen Wuornos murdered seven men here between 1989 and 1990.

   RIFODLA _____

10. Peter Sutcliffe was convicted of murdering thirteen women in this northern England town in the late 1970s.

    ROKYHEISR _____

11. The infamous Moors Murders of the 1960s involved the abduction and murder of children in this English city.

    NMAHCSERET _____

> **CURIOUS DETAIL**
>
> The United States currently has a murder rate that's roughly six times higher than that of the United Kingdom, but that wasn't always the case. US rates began to climb around the mid- to late-1800s and were forty times higher in 1974.

12. Andrew Cunanan's 1997 murder spree ended with Gianni Versace in this city.

    IMMAI HCEAB _____

13. Ed Gein committed his horrific crimes, including murder and grave robbing, here in the 1950s.

    LPINAFLDIE _____

14. Anders Behring Breivik carried out the deadliest attack in Norway's history here in 2011.

    LOSO _____

KILLER PUZZLES

CONTROVERSIAL EXECUTIONS

Identify the convicts whose death sentences ignited controversy.

ACROSS

2: On death row for his role in a 1997 Oklahoma City murder, he received multiple stays of execution.

3: His 2004 execution for murdering his three children prompted questions about the reliability of arson evidence.

5: Evidence released in 2006 cast doubt on his conviction for the fatal 1983 stabbing of a convenience store clerk.

8: His severe brain damage raised ethical questions about his execution in 1992 for the 1981 murder of a police officer.

9: His death sentence for murdering his pregnant wife, Laci, was overturned sixteen years later.

DOWN

1: Protests over recanted testimonies erupted when he was executed for killing a police officer in Georgia.

2: His Utah execution made headlines when he chose to be killed by firing squad.

4: Convicted of killing a pregnant woman and taking her baby in 2004, she was the first woman executed on US federal death row since 1953.

6: Her Texas execution after fourteen years on death row sparked debates on gender and the death penalty.

7: He was taken off death row twelve years after the Missouri Supreme Court outlawed the death penalty for minors.

CONNECTING THE DOTS

According to a study in Washington State, Black defendants are four times as likely to be sentenced to death than non-Black defendants with similar cases.

APPEL'S GALLOWS HUMOR

George Appel's last words from the electric chair in 1928 became more famous than his crime.

CURIOUS DETAIL

Appel was convicted of killing a police officer during a botched robbery. His dark pun is one of the more unusual final statements from death row.

KILLER PUZZLES

EARTH-SHATTERING CRIMES

Unscramble the words and names related to crimes that shocked the world.

1. The devastating murder of a US president in 1963 that left the nation in mourning.

   KJF SSNISASAANOIT _____

2. The 1932 crime involving a famous aviator's baby, which led to a major manhunt.

   INLDHBGER BBYA DKINPPANGI _____

3. A tragic event during a major city marathon in 2013 resulting in multiple casualties.

   TONBSO ARATHMNO BBGINOM _____

4. The unsolved murder of this six-year-old in her family's home remains one of the most infamous mysteries.

   ETBONJÉN SRYAME _____

5. In a headline-making case in the 1990s, this mother was convicted of murdering her child.

   YSECA YONTHAN _____

6. The cult who carried out a horrifying mass suicide in 1997.

   AEVHES'N TEAG _____

7. The Canadian student who killed and dismembered a young man in a gruesome 2008 case.

   KLUA GAMTTOAN _____

HISTORY—MAKING CASES

8. The crime involving the Alfred P. Murrah Federal Building in 1995.

   KOLAMAHO TIYC INBBOMG _____

9. The tragic 2012 shooting at a Connecticut elementary school.

   DYSAN OHOK _____

10. The 2000 murder of a college student at this school drew national attention to issues of domestic violence and campus safety.

    NIVUTISYRE FO SHAWNGINOT _____

11. This catastrophic 2001 terrorist attack on this day changed global security protocols.

    PESTMEREB HNEVETLE _____

12. This serial killer known for targeting women set the world on edge for decades.

    EDT NUBYD _____

13. The assassination of this prominent civil rights leader in 1965 marked a pivotal moment in US history.

    COMLLAM X _____

14. The 1999 Colorado school massacre that first sparked debates on gun control and school safety.

    COELBIMNU OTGHIONS _____

    _____

> **CONNECTING THE DOTS**
>
> In a chilling twist two months after his abduction, the Lindbergh baby was found dead just four miles from his home. The case prompted the Lindbergh Law, which made kidnapping a federal crime.

KILLER PUZZLES

RADER'S REASONING

Dennis Rader, also known as "the BTK Killer," tried to lay blame elsewhere during a 2005 interview.

A	B	C	D	E	F	G	H	I	J	K	L	M	N	O	P	Q	R	S	T	U	V	W	X	Y	Z
F															U										

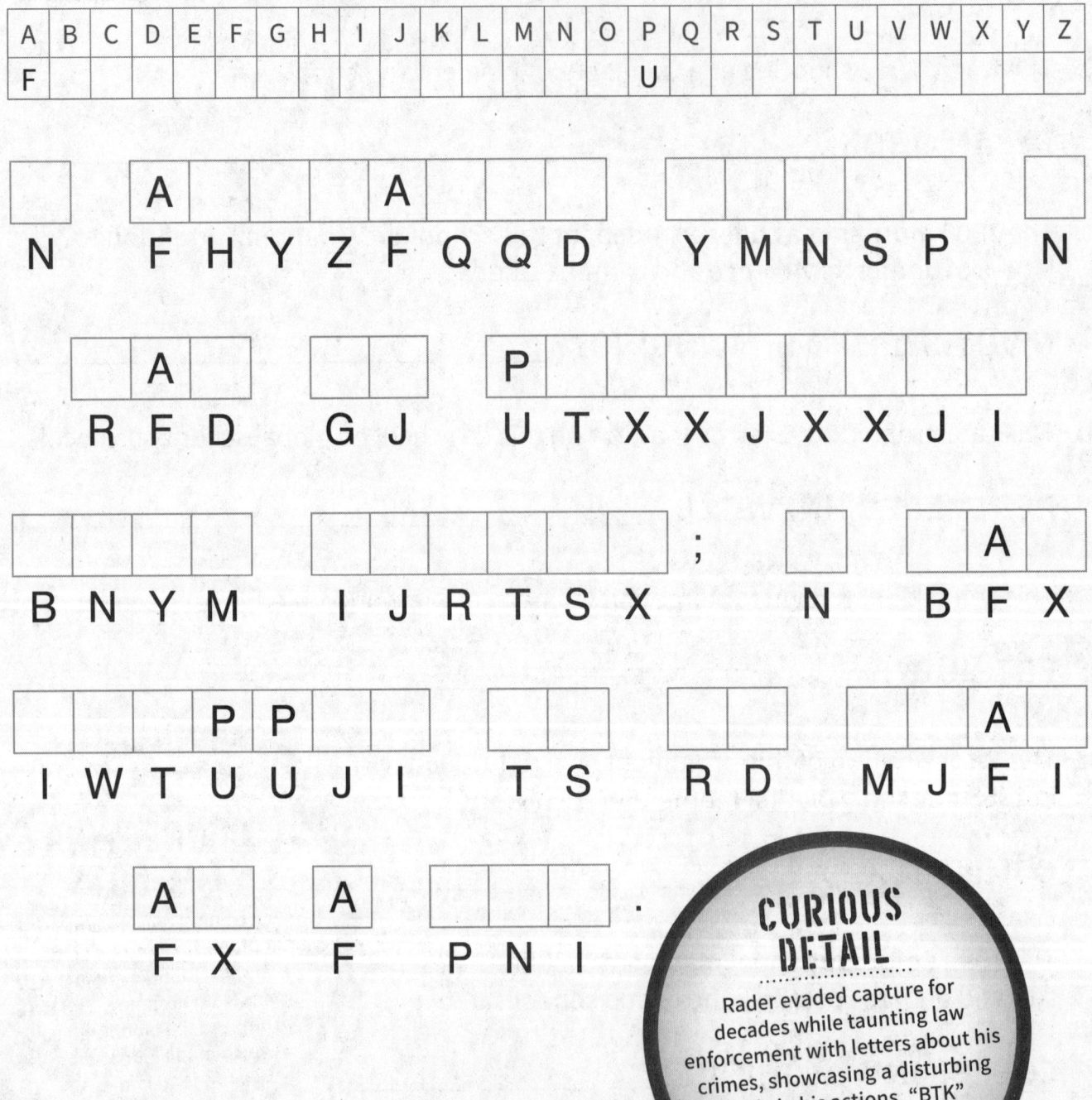

CURIOUS DETAIL

Rader evaded capture for decades while taunting law enforcement with letters about his crimes, showcasing a disturbing pride in his actions. "BTK" stood for his methods: bind, torture, kill.

KILLER NICKNAMES

These are the kinds of descriptors you'll find in all the most notorious aliases.

```
T T L B N R C W R Y R K
L N B J O L E E O E L K
K B D A O M K P N D I M
S U R W C L B O P L I M
M T N E A K I E L I T W
U C R T Y T P E R N R R
R H S A U A R A A W E R
D E Y C N E L M C T B T
E R E X A G E S N K T D
R X L P Z C L U Y R E N
E D E N I N H E J B R R
R R W R Y N B K R M P Z
```

Killer	Bomber	Slayer
Stalker	Widow	Reaper
Strangler	Ripper	Hunter
Butcher	Iceman	Executioner
Clown	Backpacker	Murderer

HISTORY—MAKING CASES

135

KILLER PUZZLES

MASTERS OF ESCAPE

Match each criminal to their escape description.

1. Billy the Kid
2. El Chapo
3. D. B. Cooper
4. Frank Abagnale
5. Richard Lee McNair
6. John Dillinger
7. Ronnie Biggs
8. John Anglin
9. Richard Matt
10. Ted Bundy
11. Rédoine Faïd
12. Michel Vaujour
13. Brady Kilpatrick
14. Ronald Silva
15. Henri Charrière

A. EXPLOSIVES
B. PEANUT BUTTER
C. DISGUISED AS PRISON GUARD
D. FROM NEW MEXICO JAIL
E. HELICOPTER
F. THROUGH COURTHOUSE WINDOW
G. IMPERSONATED POLICE OFFICER
H. LADDER
I. THROUGH A PIPE
J. LIP BALM
K. TUNNELED OUT
L. RAFT
M. HIJACKED PLANE
N. BOAT
O. DRESSED IN WIFE'S CLOTHES

CONNECTING THE DOTS

In 1962, the Anglin brothers created dummies to place in their beds to deceive guards while they made their escape. They used materials like raincoats for the dummies' bodies and human hair for the heads, leaving the guards none the wiser until morning.

KILLER RECALL

Test your true-crime knowledge with a quick chapter quiz.

1. True or false: Jeffery Dahmer was executed by lethal injection in 1994.
   _____

2. How did Ted Bundy escape after his first capture?
   _____

3. In what public place did James Holmes famously open fire, killing twelve people?
   _____

4. Which band did Charles Manson help write a song for?
   _____

5. Where was the site of the 1929 St. Valentine's Day Massacre?
   _____

6. Which famous fashion designer was killed in Miami in 1997?
   _____

7. True or false: The United States sees more murders each year than the United Kingdom?
   _____

8. What age was Christopher Simmons when he was executed for murder in Missouri?
   _____

9. A famous 1932 kidnapping led to the establishment of what legislation?
   _____

10. Dennis Rader referred to himself as "the BTK Killer," which stood for what?
    _____

HISTORY—MAKING CASES

SHOCKING STALKERS

KILLER PUZZLES

MILESTONES IN STALKING PREVENTION

Stalking wasn't always considered a crime—reveal what changed that.

ACROSS

6: This country introduced stricter stalking laws after the 2006 murder of journalist Anna Politkovskaya.

7: In 1989, Rebecca Shaeffer's murder led to this state creating the first anti-stalking law.

8: Anti-stalking laws in this country were introduced after Shiori Ino's death in 1999.

9: The country where the Protection from Harassment Act was enacted in 1997.

10: The first state to introduce criminal penalties for stalking after the murder of Linda Yalem in 1990.

CONNECTING THE DOTS

The tragic murder of actress Rebecca Schaeffer by an obsessed fan in 1989 led to the first anti-stalking laws in the United States, sparking nationwide reforms.

DOWN

1: Ruling against Scott Paul Bouters helped this state enact a comprehensive stalking law in 1992.

2: The first anti-stalking law in Australia was passed in this state in 1994.

3: The federal act that introduced penalties for stalking across state lines in 1994.

4: In 1999, this US state became one of the first to pass a cyberstalking law.

5: This country enacted the Safe Spaces Act, a law that targets gender-based sexual harassment and cyberstalking, in 2019.

LEGAL BOUNDARIES

Match the legal lingo with its abbreviated definitions.

1. Harassment
2. Restraining Order
3. Menacing
4. Victim
5. GPS
6. Cyberstalking
7. Emotional Distress
8. Injunction
9. Prevention Order
10. Incident Report
11. Surveillance
12. Aggravated
13. Monitoring
14. Victim Advocacy
15. Trespassing

A. ORDER TO PREVENT CONTACT
B. CAUSING FEAR OR DISTRESS
C. ELECTRONIC STALKING
D. FOLLOWING SOMEONE
E. CLOSE OBSERVATION
F. THREATS OR INTIMIDATION
G. ORDER TO DETER STALKING
H. UNAUTHORIZED ENTRY
I. PSYCHOLOGICAL IMPACT
J. ENHANCED STALKING
K. PERSON BEING STALKED
L. DETAILED INCIDENT DESCRIPTION
M. TRACKING DEVICE
N. LEGAL AND EMOTIONAL SUPPORT
O. ORDER TO STOP

CURIOUS DETAIL

Approximately 76 percent of women killed by an intimate partner had been stalked by that partner prior to their death, indicating that stalking behavior is a significant warning sign that can lead to fatal outcomes.

KILLER PUZZLES

CORBETT'S DELUSION

In this notebook entry, Sandra Bullock's stalker, Joshua Corbett, showcased the mental acrobatics stalkers can do to convince themselves they have a relationship—or are owed one—with their victim.

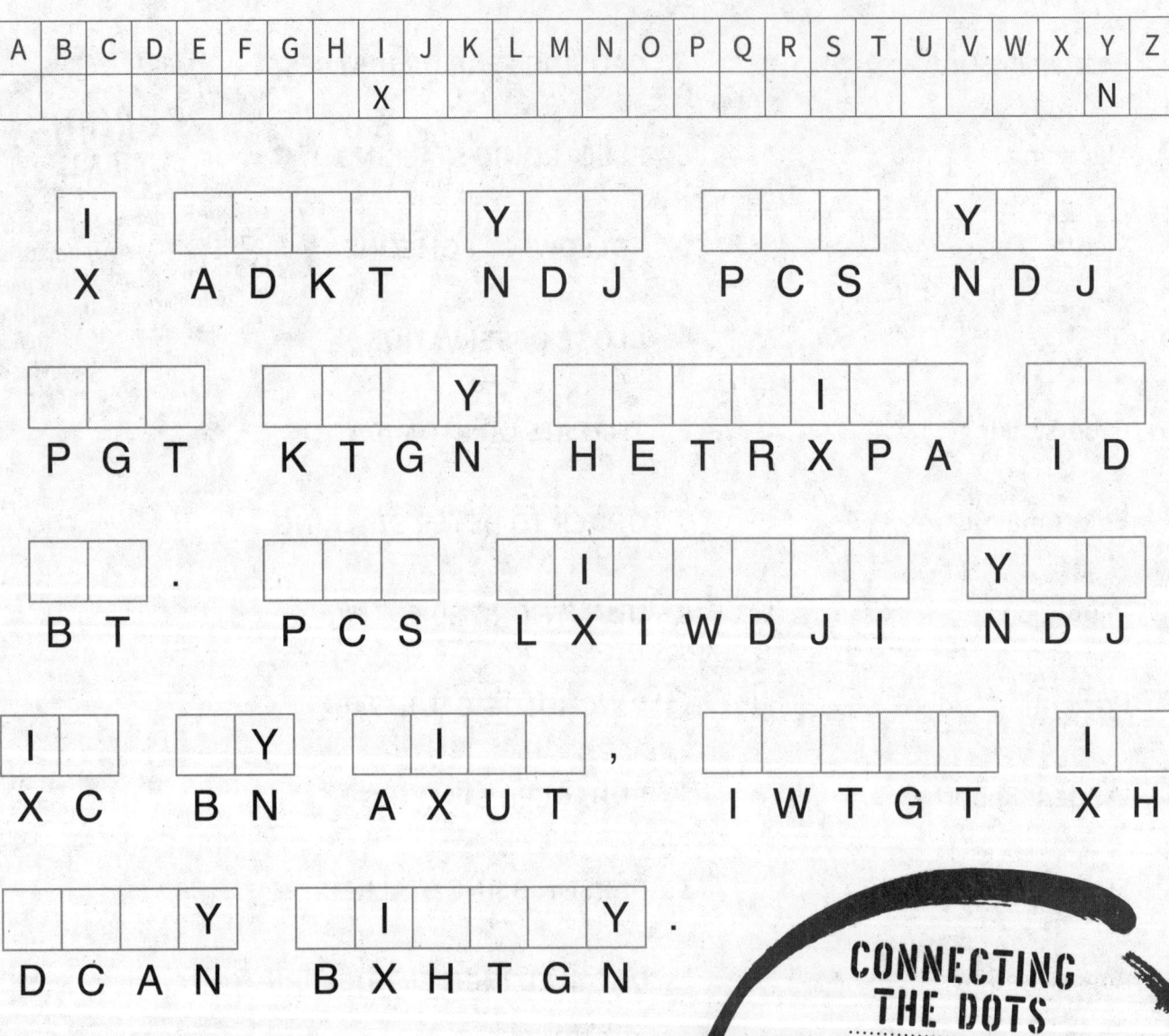

CONNECTING THE DOTS

Authorities found evidence in Corbett's notebook that he'd intended to sexually assault the actress, and surveillance saw him lurking outside her home for three days before he broke in. Bullock called 9-1-1 from inside a locked wardrobe while he banged on her bedroom door.

PSYCHOLOGICAL PROFILES

Analyze the grid for the psychological terms related to stalking cases.

```
N O I S S E S B O P Y N Q A
I S O L A T I O N A R R M G
R M D W L J A N G M Q U Y D
T L A R C N G G D M A Y D K
F N Y N X O R V S R T P T T
E G E I I E M I T I N N Q V
A N E M S P S P V N E D P N
R T O S S S U I U M Z A M C
Y T I I I S S L H L R T O B
P O X C S L A C A A S N N T
N M R D U U A R N T T I T N
K A G P B T L O A R I R O M
N L M D T L I E O H B O V N
Z I J A Q A B L D V Q M N P
```

Obsession	Control	Anxiety
Paranoia	Narcissism	Impulsivity
Delusion	Isolation	Harassment
Manipulation	Fear	Compulsion
Attachment	Aggression	Trauma

KILLER PUZZLES

FAME AND FEAR

Unscramble the names of celebrities who have experienced stalking incidents.

1. The actress was murdered by her stalker, Robert John Bardo, in 1989.

   CCABERE CHASERFFE _____

2. A stalker attempted to break into this former Disney star's home multiple times in 2019.

   MEDI OOLTAV _____

3. Stalker John Hinckley, Jr. attempted to assassinate President Ronald Reagan to win this actress's love.

   JIEOD SFORET _____

4. The "Queen of Rock 'n' Roll" who dealt with an obsessive fan who would show up at her home.

   NATI RUTRNE _____

5. This pop icon had multiple stalkers, including a man who broke into her London home in 2011.

   DAMNONA _____

6. This music legend was shot and killed by his stalker, Mark David Chapman, in 1980.

   HOJN NENLON _____

7. This *Twilight* actress said in 2012 she had "one crazy stalker" but wasn't letting him intimidate her.

   NETRKSI WETSATR _____

8. The *Black Widow* actress filed a restraining order against her stalker, who believes he fathered her son.

   RACSTELT HOJNAOSSN _____

SHOCKING STALKERS

9. Alexander Kardalian was arrested after showing up at this singer's home multiple times following his release from prison.

   YILME YCSUR _____

10. This *Back to the Future* actor received thousands of threatening letters from stalker Tina Marie Ledbetter.

    HEACLMI J OXF _____

11. This pop star had a stalker who wanted to castrate him (out of love).

    UJSNIT BBEIRE _____

12. New York police arrested a stalker of this Pennsylvania-born music icon for trying to break into her apartment.

    YATROL WSITF _____

13. The "Soak Up the Sun" singer faced a stalker who believed they were soulmates and showed up at her parents' home.

    RLYHSE ORWC _____

14. This actress needed protection from online stalking after her accounts were hacked while filming *Phoenix Rising*.

    VANE CHARLE ODOW _____
    _____

15. One man was arrested twice in one week in 2014 for stalking this singer and murder-mystery actress.

    ELSEAN MOGZE _____
    _____

> **CURIOUS DETAIL**
> Romantic comedies have caught heat in recent years for romanticizing the idea of pursuit. The Netflix thriller *You* took things a step further and faced criticism for romanticizing actual stalking. Its star, Penn Badgley, urged fans not to sympathize with his criminal character.

FATAL OBSESSIONS

Complete the crossword with the names of stalkers whose obsessions led to murder—successfully or attempted.

ACROSS
1: The stalker convicted of stabbing actress Theresa Saldana in 1982.
4: (2 wds.) He blamed his assassination attempt on Jodie Foster and the movie *Taxi Driver*.
6: The ex-husband of Tonya Harding, he helped orchestrate the attack on Nancy Kerrigan.
9: The stalker who murdered famous fashion designer Gianni Versace.
10: He stalked and murdered actress Rebecca Schaeffer in 1989.

CONNECTING THE DOTS

Christina Grimmie's stalker had been obsessed with her for years but had no criminal record. On the night of the shooting, he traveled from another state, armed with multiple weapons he'd purchased just days earlier.

DOWN
2: The former fan club president who stalked and eventually murdered singer Selena in 1995.
3: He stalked John Lennon for months before killing him.
5: He was convicted in the shooting death of actress Lana Clarkson in 2003.
7: Singer Christina Grimmie was shot and killed by this stalker at a concert in 2016.
8: Guitarist Dimebag Darrell was killed onstage by this stalker.

GRASSO'S LAST GROUSE

Despite receiving four dozen steamed mussels and clams, a double cheeseburger, a half-dozen barbecued spareribs, and two strawberry milkshakes for his last meal, stalker and murderer Thomas J. Grasso was not pleased with this substitution.

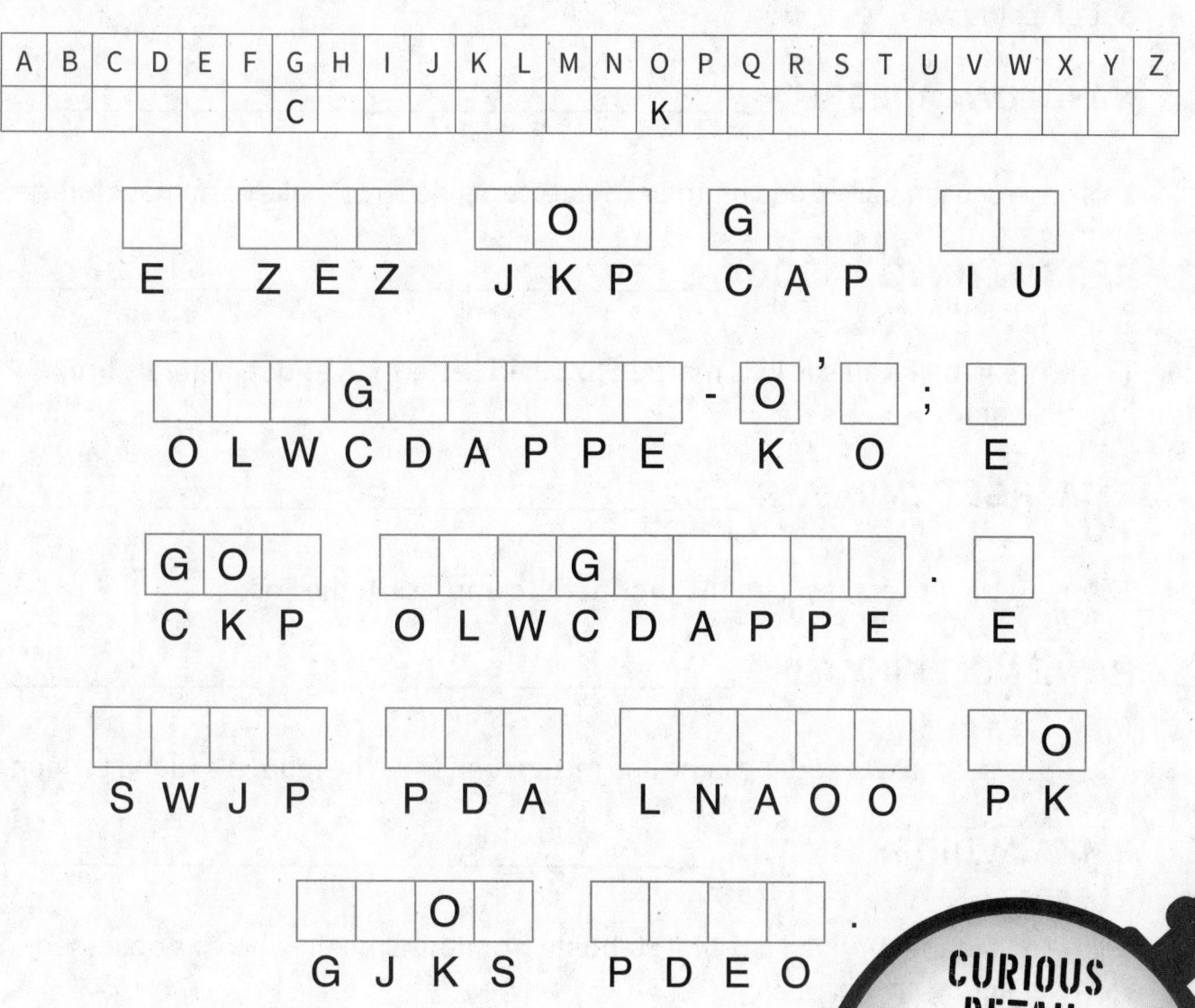

KILLER PUZZLES

NAMING NAMES

Unscramble the names of these obsessive and unstable stalkers.

1. Selena was stalked and murdered by this woman, her fan club president, out of jealousy.

   NAYDLOA LADRSÍVA _____

2. This obsessed fan stalked and murdered Rebecca Schaeffer to make her famous forever.

   RERBTO HNJO BAROD _____

3. This woman believed she was married to David Letterman and repeatedly broke into his home.

   RMAARGET YMRA AYR _____

4. This man tried to assassinate the president to impress Jodie Foster.

   HONJ NCLEKIHY RJ _____

5. This obsessed fan was seeking fame and recognition when he murdered John Lennon.

   RMKA AVDID PCHMANA _____

6. Theresa Saldana survived a brutal stabbing from this stalker, who was obsessed with her acting career.

   RTAUHR JNAKOSC _____

7. This man broke into Sandra Bullock's home because he believed she was his wife.

   SJOHUA RTEBCTO _____

SHOCKING STALKERS

8. Björk was stalked by this man, who sent her a letter bomb.

   ACORDRI PLZEÓ _____

9. This stalker threatened to kill Madonna because he believed she was meant to be his wife.

   RBRTOE YDEWE SNKHOIS _____
   _____

10. This stalker left disturbing items outside of Keira Knightley's home.

    KARM LEVRLI _____

11. Shawn Johnson's stalker, who traveled cross-country intending to kidnap her, believing they were meant to be together.

    RTOBER RANYO _____

12. Gwyneth Paltrow's stalker, who sent her hundreds of disturbing letters and packages, professing his love for her.

    ETDNA CHEAMLI IOSU _____

13. One of Selena Gomez's stalkers, who threatened to kill her due to obsessive infatuation.

    OTMHAS DRCONIBKI _____

14. The man who threatened Congresswoman Pramila Jayapal outside of her home in 2022.

    TERBT FLOSREL _____

> **CONNECTING THE DOTS**
>
> Drew Barrymore's stalker, Chad Michael Busto, also attempted to stalk Emma Watson. Despite his history of bizarre behavior, it was not until he entered a dressing room at New York Fashion Week demanding to see Watson that he was officially put behind bars.

KILLER PUZZLES

MAUDSLEY'S DEFENSE

Nicknamed "the Real Hannibal," Robert John Maudsley's rationale for stalking and killing his victims would be almost philanthropic if it weren't sadistic and delusional.

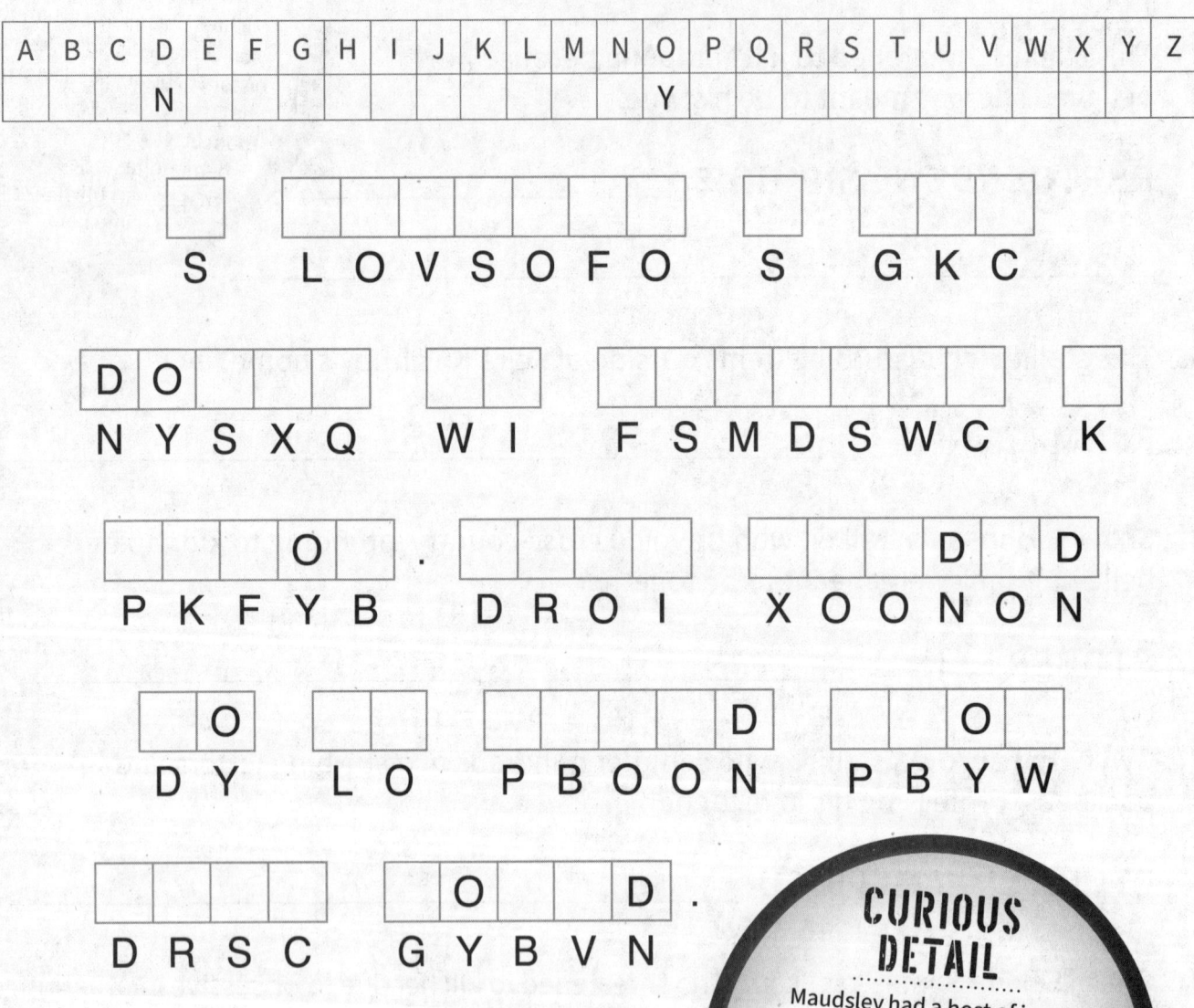

SUPPORT FOR VICTIMS

Recover the words related to resources available for stalking victims.

```
R E D R O G N I N I A R T S E R
N E M P O W E R M E N T L N N Y
O S D G Y C A C O V D A T R M M
I L S R N D R S S H N R L L Z T
T B J E M I A E O H O L V Z B V
N M Y L N F L T P P E R J X M P
E D B P E E L E P O E L L W Z M
V T E T A I R U S D R Z T L R Y
R S Y F N R S A U N Z T T E M K
E N H E E L E C W T U G I R R V
T X K E A N A H P A N O T N Y Z
N Z Y G L T S R T B G X C Y G N
I R E T I T R E Z G N X D L L Q
T L L O Y N E B V Y Q G M Q J J
Y V N R V V B R P V T R B D N J
```

Hotline	Safety	Awareness
Counseling	Shelter	Intervention
Therapy	Education	Shelter
Restraining Order	Legal Support	Reporting
Advocacy	Defense	Empowerment

POP CULTURE PREDATORS

Connect each fictional stalker to their story.

1. Joe Goldberg
2. Annie Wilkes
3. Buffalo Bill
4. Norman Bates
5. Rachel Watson
6. Adrian Griffin
7. Freddy Krueger
8. Sam Coulson
9. Alex Forrest
10. Amy Dunne
11. Teddy Gammell
12. Daniel Wheeler
13. Peter Foley
14. Billy Loomis
15. Seymour Parish

A. *THE GIRL ON THE TRAIN*
B. *THE INVISIBLE MAN*
C. *SCREAM*
D. *THE BODYGUARD*
E. *YOU*
F. *MISERY*
G. *ONE HOUR PHOTO*
H. *FATAL ATTRACTION*
I. *NEVER BEEN KISSED*
J. *SILENCE OF THE LAMBS*
K. *MEMENTO*
L. *PSYCHO*
M. *COPYCAT*
N. *GONE GIRL*
O. *A NIGHTMARE ON ELM STREET*

CONNECTING THE DOTS

Following *Fatal Attraction*'s release in 1987, the term "bunny boiler" became synonymous with obsessive behavior.

SHOCKING STALKERS

KILLER RECALL

Test your true-crime knowledge with a quick chapter quiz.

1. Which US state enacted the country's first anti-stalking law?

   _____

2. What term did UK defense lawyers use in high-profile stalking cases in the 1990s?

   _____

3. What is the legal term for the psychological impact of stalking?

   _____

4. True or false: Most women killed by an intimate partner have been stalked by that partner prior to their death.

   _____

5. Which famous actress shared a stalker with a US president?

   _____

6. Which stalker believed she was married to David Letterman?

   _____

7. What was the name of the stalker convicted of stabbing Theresa Saldana?

   _____

8. True or false: Christina Grimmie's killer had only been stalking her for a few months before the murder.

   _____

9. Which English murderer was nicknamed "the Real Hannibal"?

   _____

10. Which 1987 film coined the term "bunny boiler"?

    _____

MASS MURDERERS

KILLER PUZZLES

NAMES BEHIND THE HEADLINES

Fill in the names of the infamous figures responsible for these mass murders.

ACROSS

2: The Bath School bomber who killed forty-five people in 1927.
4: The perpetrator of the Oklahoma City bombing that killed 168 people in 1995.
8: The gunman who killed fifty-eight people during a Las Vegas music festival in 2017.
9: He killed nine worshippers during a church service in Charleston in 2015.
10: He opened fire at a Florida nightclub in 2016, killing forty-nine people.

CONNECTING THE DOTS

The Virginia Tech shooter sent a multimedia package to NBC News between his attacks. It included a video statement, photographs, and writings expressing his bizarre grievances, mostly against the wealthy.

DOWN

1: He killed seventy-seven people in a 2011 massacre in Norway.
3: The Texas Tower shooter who killed seventeen people in 1966.
5: One of the two Columbine High School shooters responsible for thirteen deaths in 1999.
6: The Virginia Tech shooter who killed thirty-two people in 2007.
7: He was responsible for the Sandy Hook Elementary School shooting, claiming twenty-six lives in 2012.

MASS MURDERERS

THE AFTERMATH

Link the actions taken with the infamous events that prompted them.

1. Gun control
2. Increased school security
3. National mourning
4. Anti-terrorism legislation
5. Mental health initiatives
6. Background checks
7. Media scrutiny
8. Victim compensation
9. Police training
10. Community outreach
11. Activism for gun reform
12. Psych evaluations
13. Emergency response revisions
14. Memorials
15. Mental health awareness

A. TORONTO VAN ATTACK
B. BATON ROUGE POLICE SHOOTING
C. OKLAHOMA CITY BOMBING
D. COLUMBINE SHOOTING
E. NORWAY MASSACRE
F. LAS VEGAS SHOOTING
G. VIRGINIA TECH SHOOTING
H. AURORA THEATER SHOOTING
I. PARKLAND SCHOOL SHOOTING
J. PLANNED PARENTHOOD SHOOTING
K. PULSE NIGHTCLUB SHOOTING
L. TEXAS TOWER SHOOTING
M. AUSTRALIA MOSQUE SHOOTING
N. SANDY HOOK SHOOTING
O. CHARLESTON CHURCH SHOOTING

CURIOUS DETAIL

After the Sandy Hook shooting, schools across the country implemented heightened security measures, including controlled access points and active shooter drills. Even so, there have been more than 200 school shootings since then.

KILLER PUZZLES

CHO'S JUSTIFICATION

Between two shooting sprees in 2007, Seung-Hui Cho sent a video to news outlets that gave this haunting (and self-pitying) explanation.

A	B	C	D	E	F	G	H	I	J	K	L	M	N	O	P	Q	R	S	T	U	V	W	X	Y	Z
														A					F						

☐ O ☐   ☐ O ☐ ☐ ☐   ☐ ☐
K A G   R A D O Q P   Y Q

☐ ☐ T O ☐   ☐ O ☐ ☐ ☐ .
U Z F A M   O A D Z Q D

☐ ☐ ☐   ☐ ☐ ☐ ☐ ' T
K A G   P U P Z   F

☐ ☐ ☐ ☐ ☐ ☐ T ☐ ☐ ☐
G Z P Q D E F M Z P

☐ ☐ .
Y Q

CONNECTING THE DOTS

Following the Virginia Tech shooting, authorities discovered that Seung-Hui Cho had untreated mental health issues, including anxiety and depression, highlighting the role of mental illness in violent tragedies.

MASS MURDERERS

PUBLIC REACTION

Search for the things that follow every modern mass murder.

```
I B C B I B M O W E R M R M
T N J O X N U E V P L B S J
H M V V V T T I M G D I J L
G J B E R E T E N O L L J R
I J C A S A R I R A R J J A
L P G O R T T A N V H I F D
T E U R M R I O G E I T A S
O L A B O M I G A E E E I L
P N I P L T E D A R J S W M
S N E G A I L N M T Y N N S
B R J S I I C A T L I N G P
R K N T N V T I A A R O D D
Z E J E K H J N T N R Q N T
S Z S T N Q A J Q Y Z Y W T
```

Sensationalism	Reporting	Aftermath
Coverage	Headlines	Spotlight
Analysis	Publicity	Investigation
Vigil	Interviews	Narrative
Memorial	Commentary	Outrage

KILLER PUZZLES

UNDER THE RADAR

Can you decode the identities of these lesser-known killers?

1. He perpetrated the 2007 Omaha mall shooting, killing eight people.

   BERROT SWIKNAH _____

2. He was responsible for the 1982 massacre at a Miami welding shop, killing eight workers.

   ALRC NOBWR _____

3. In a school shooting at an Australian university in 2002, he killed two people and injured five.

   NUAH NUY NXAGI _____

4. This 1993 Long Island Railroad shooter killed six people and injured nineteen.

   NILOC NUGSERFO _____

5. The 1986 Edmond post office shooter who killed fourteen postal workers.

   TKIRPAC LHRLIESR _____

6. This pilot deliberately crashed his plane in an act of suicide, killing all 150 people on board the Germanwings flight.

   SADENAR TBZUIL _____

7. He killed eight coworkers in a 2010 shooting at a Manchester, Connecticut, beer distributor.

   ARMO NTOHR _____

MASS MURDERERS

8. He carried out the 2011 Seal Beach salon shooting, killing eight people.

   TCTSO ARDKEIA _____

9. He killed three when he opened fire at a Colorado Planned Parenthood clinic in 2015.

   BETROR AERD _____

10. He shot and killed five people in Washington's Cascade Mall in 2016.

    CRANA TICNE _____

11. The Filipino sailor who killed all forty-four people on his Pacific Air Lines flight in 1964 by shooting both pilots, causing the plane to crash.

    AFCNCIORS AULPA ZOEGSANL _____
    _____

12. He killed seven coworkers in a 1999 Honolulu office shooting.

    NAYRB UIGSUEY _____

13. This man killed six people in the 2014 Isla Vista shootings in California.

    LITEOL DGROER _____

14. He killed four people in 2018 at a Tennessee Waffle House.

    VSATRI INKRNIEG _____
    _____

CURIOUS DETAIL
Many mass murderers choose suicide to avoid capture; studies show that around 30 percent of them take their own lives at the scene or shortly after.

NOTHING NEW

Mass murder is nothing new. Uncover the names of these killers from decades past.

ACROSS

1: He murdered thirteen people in a twelve-minute shooting spree in Camden, New Jersey, in 1949.
5: This German teacher murdered his family before setting several fires and shooting twenty people in 1913.
8: The bodies of six men he'd murdered were found buried on his North Dakota farm in 1915.
9: This former merchant seaman shot up a Texas chain restaurant after driving his car into it in 1991, killing twenty-three people.
10: He smuggled a time bomb onto an ammunition barge in City Point, Virginia, during the Civil War, killing 43 people and wounding 126 more.

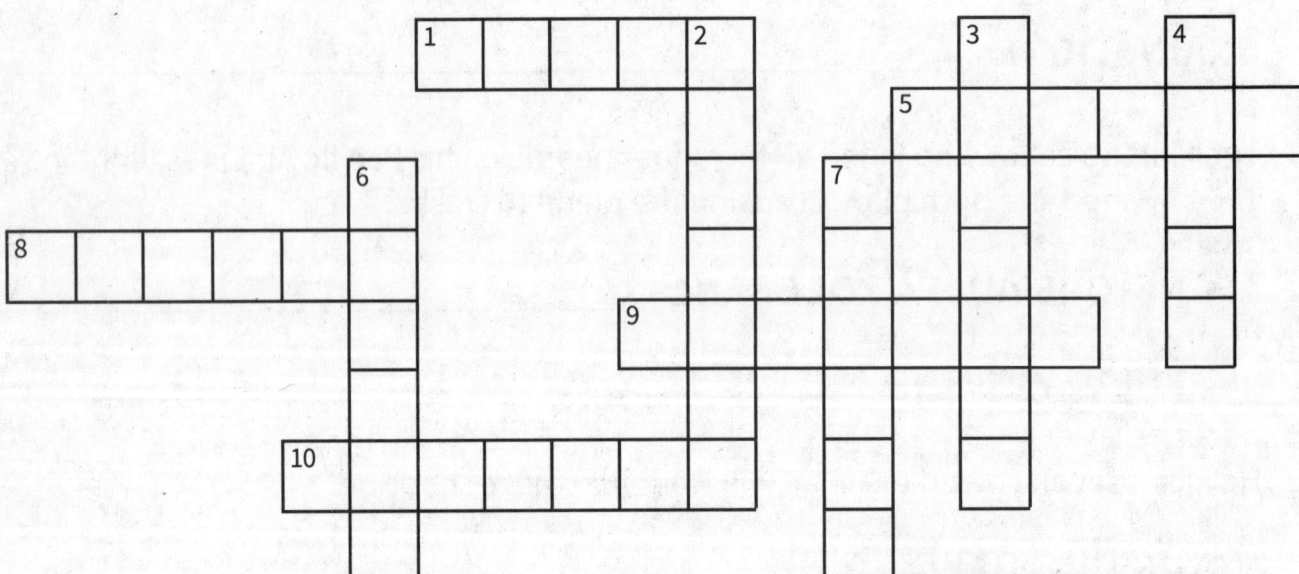

DOWN

2: He murdered twelve family members in Texas in 1926 after a dispute.
3: He confessed to killing more than twenty people, including six men aboard a ship in 1920.
4: He killed forty-five people, mostly children, in the 1927 Bath School bombing.
6: He planted a dynamite time bomb on a United Airlines Flight in 1955, killing forty-four people on board.
7: This prisoner killed twenty-one men after setting fire to a city lockup in 1977.

CONNECTING THE DOTS

From 1982 to 2024, only 4 mass shootings were carried out by women, while 145 were carried out by men. And although school shootings by students have become more common, the average age of mass shooters is thirty-three.

MCVEIGH'S PHILOSOPHY

Perpetrator of the Oklahoma City bombing Timothy McVeigh quoted this stanza (somewhat ironically) before being executed by the state of Indiana.

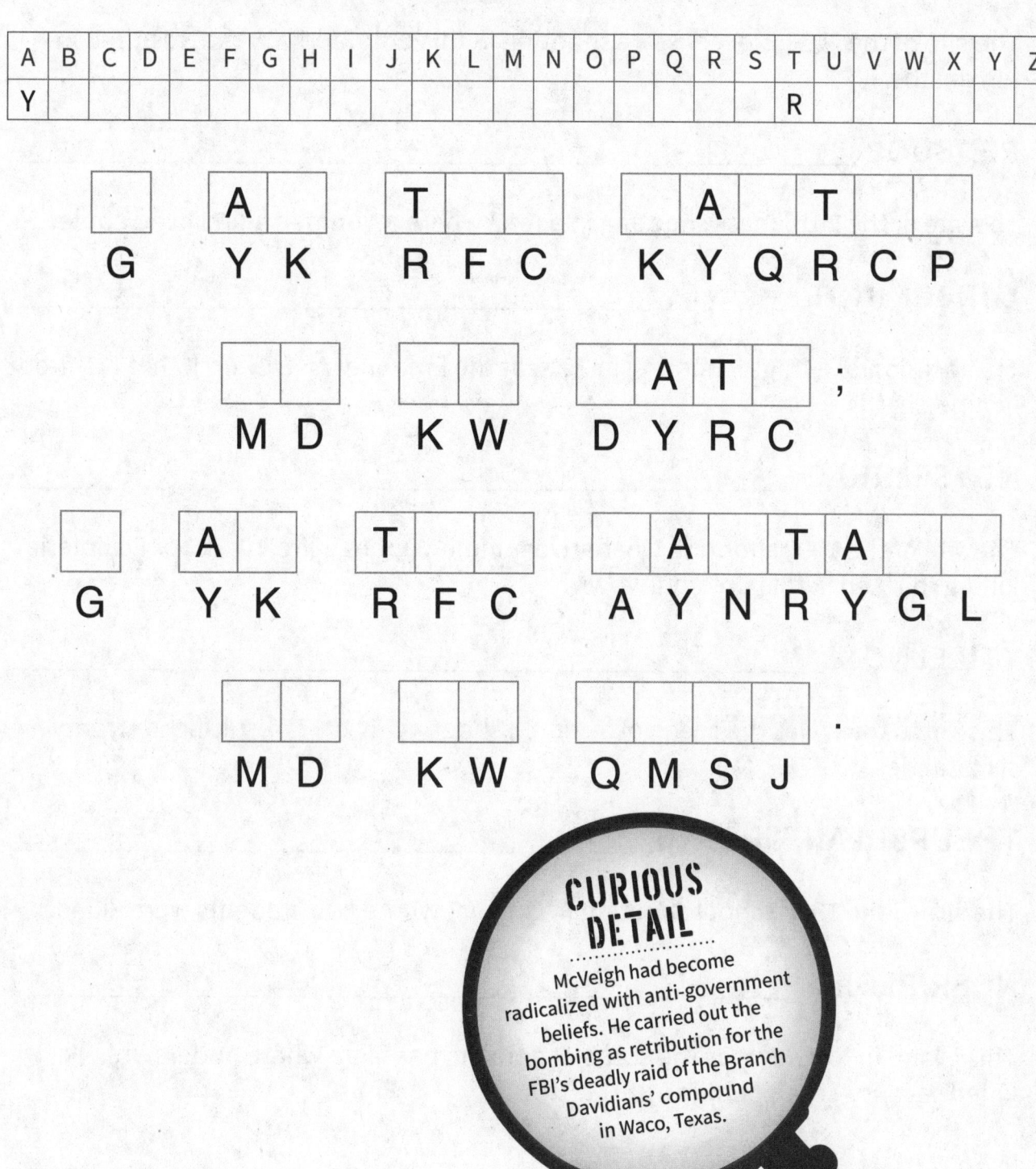

KILLER PUZZLES

SITES OF HORROR

Based on the clues provided, match the location of the mass murder to the description of the infamous event.

1. The site of the 2021 grocery store shooting in this Colorado city that resulted in ten deaths.

   REDBUOL _____

2. The site of the 2016 mass shooting in a mall where a gunman killed five people.

   LURBGNINOT _____

3. The location of a tragic shooting in 2015 at the Emanuel AME Church that resulted in nine deaths.

   NOTSELRHAC _____

4. The site of the 1999 shooting where two gunmen opened fire in a school cafeteria killing thirteen in this Colorado town.

   TTILELNOT _____

5. This Texas town was the scene of a church shooting in 2017, resulting in twenty-six fatalities.

   THEURSDLAN RIPSSNG _____

6. The site of the 1998 school shooting in Oregon, where two students were killed.

   NGSRIPLDIEF _____

7. This island in Norway was the scene of a tragic massacre where Anders Breivik killed seventy-seven people in 2011.

   YØATU DNSIAL _____

MASS MURDERERS

8. This city in Florida was home to the Pulse nightclub, where a gunman killed forty-nine people in a targeted attack in 2016.

   ROLNAOD _____

9. This Colorado city was the scene of a tragic 2012 theater shooting, where twelve people were killed.

   RROAUA _____

10. This California city saw James Huberty kill twenty-one people at a McDonald's in 1984.

    NSA OIDRSY _____

11. This New Zealand city was the site of the 2019 mosque shootings, resulting in fifty-one fatalities.

    TSHCRIRUCHHC _____

12. Dual bombings in 1998 targeted US embassies in these two East African countries.

    NEKAY NATZNIAA _____

13. The site of a mass shooting at a Walmart in Texas in 2019 that resulted in twenty-three deaths.

    LE SPAO _____

14. The location of the 2018 shooting at a synagogue in Pennsylvania, where eleven worshippers were killed.

    TISPTGHURB _____

CONNECTING THE DOTS

The states with the highest number of mass shootings include California, Texas, and Florida. California, in particular, has seen some of the deadliest mass shootings in US history.

KILLER PUZZLES

HARRIS AND KLEBOLD'S GOALS

Tape recordings of a conversation between Columbine shooters Eric Harris and Dylan Klebold in the month before the mass murder revealed their disturbing desires and lack of remorse.

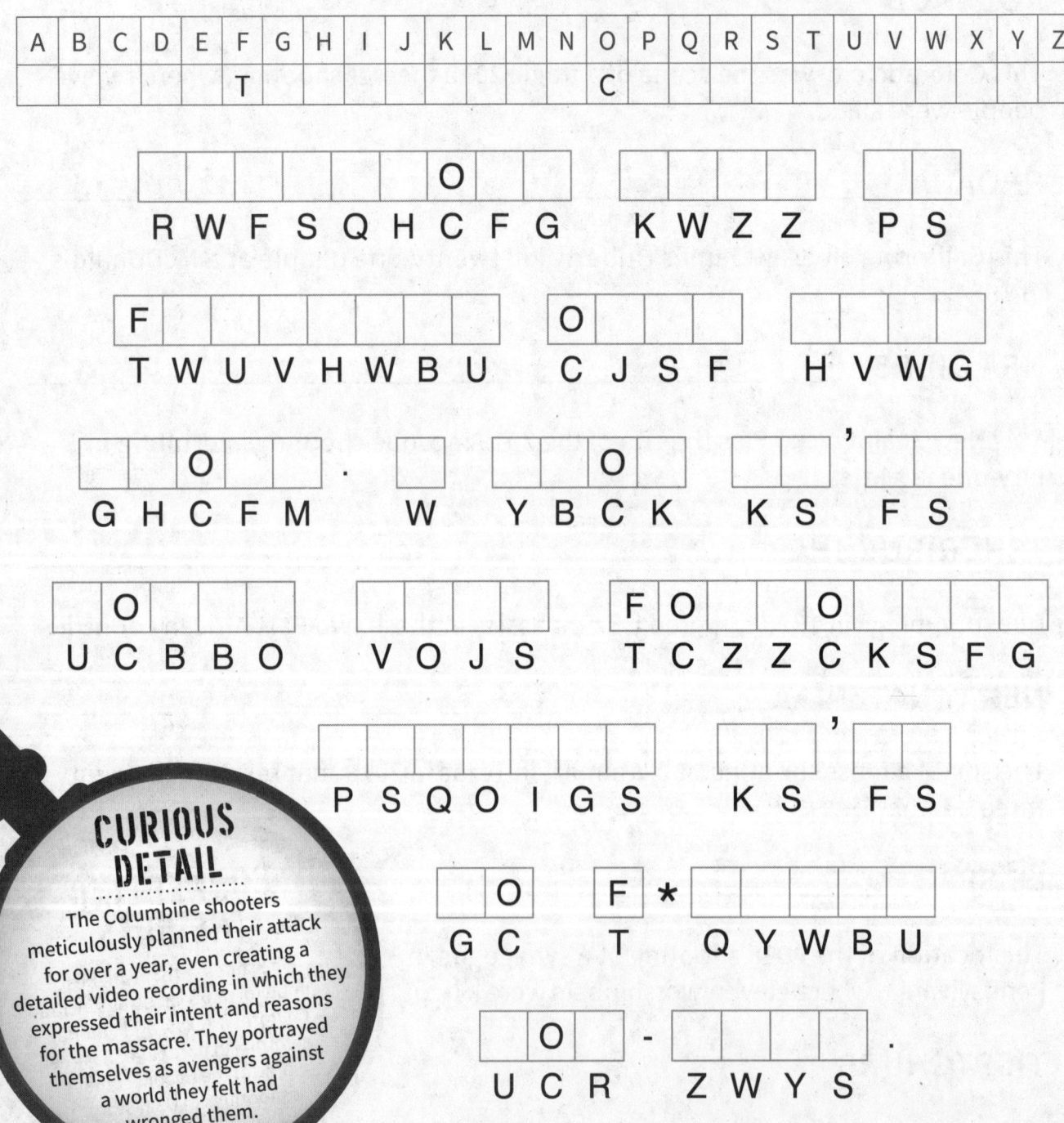

CURIOUS DETAIL

The Columbine shooters meticulously planned their attack for over a year, even creating a detailed video recording in which they expressed their intent and reasons for the massacre. They portrayed themselves as avengers against a world they felt had wronged them.

NO REGRETS

Reveal the mass murderers who displayed no remorse for their actions.

```
N M M B Z K K J N R Z M M
A X D J F Y I A P M Q Q Z
M W R T V O I V X W R Q Z
T Y L M B S O S I Z U R C
I G L Y S T Y R I E P T K
H B P A N L J T M R R T V
W G N A P Q W C R D R B Q
W I Y Z J A V N L E S A N
M R A Z Y E D O R E B E H
B D R Z I Q B D M K E U X
D N M G N E Y L O T C Y H
Q R H K L A O B A C Y H X
B D Y K Q H L M J R K J O
```

McVeigh	Paddock	Holmes
Breivik	Bryant	Mateen
Huberty	Cho	Lanza
Harris	Roof	Klebold
Whitman	Cruz	Minassian

KILLER PUZZLES

PROFILES IN CRIMINALITY

Match the notorious mass murderers to the psychological disorders ascribed to them.

1. Ted Bundy
2. Gavin Long
3. Albert Fish
4. Jared Loughner
5. James Holmes
6. Chris Dorner
7. Dylan Klebold
8. Anders Behring Breivik
9. Edmund Kemper
10. John Wayne Gacy
11. Robert Bowers
12. Jeffrey Dahmer
13. Dylann Roof
14. Richard Ramirez
15. Nikolas Cruz

A. NECROPHILIA
B. MOOD DISORDER
C. BORDERLINE PERSONALITY DISORDER
D. PSYCHOPATHY
E. PARANOID PERSONALITY DISORDER
F. NARCISSISTIC PERSONALITY DISORDER
G. SCHIZOTYPAL PERSONALITY DISORDER
H. DELUSIONAL DISORDER
I. SADISM
J. ANTISOCIAL PERSONALITY DISORDER
K. PARANOID SCHIZOPHRENIA
L. FETAL ALCOHOL SYNDROME
M. PARAPHILIA
N. DEPRESSION
O. DELUSIONAL DISORDER

CONNECTING THE DOTS

According to a study from Columbia University, approximately 25 percent of mass shootings are associated with nonpsychotic psychiatric or neurological illnesses such as depression or substance abuse.

KILLER RECALL

Test your true-crime knowledge with a quick chapter quiz.

1. Who was the mass murderer responsible for the Norway Massacre?

   _____

2. What effect did the Toronto Van Attack have?

   _____

3. Which shooting prompted the implementation of heightened security measures in schools?

   _____

4. Who killed forty-four people on a United Airlines flight in 1955?

   _____

5. A movie theater shooting in what Colorado municipality killed twelve people?

   _____

6. What percentage of mass murderers take their own lives at the scene or shortly after?

   _____

7. True or false: Men are far more likely to commit mass murder than women.

   _____

8. Which Florida city was home to the Pulse nightclub?

   _____

9. True or false: The Columbine shooters planned their attack for just a month before carrying it out.

   _____

10. James Holmes suffered from which severe mental disorder?

    _____

SOLUTIONS

SERIAL KILLERS

TELLTALE HEARTS (AND OTHER THINGS)

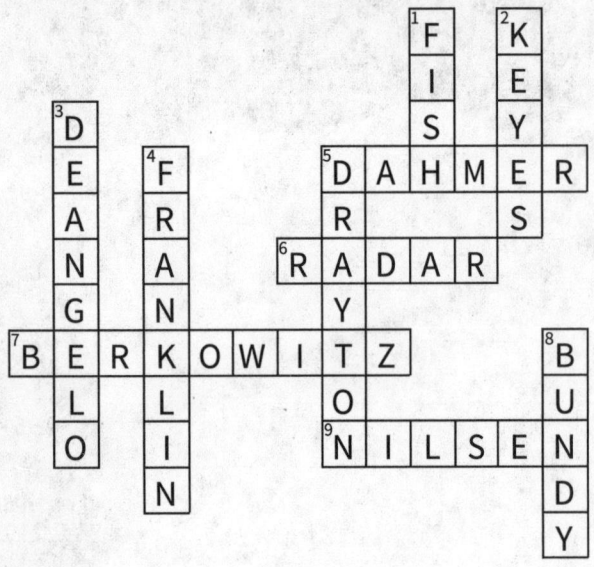

TRUE-CRIME CATCHWORDS

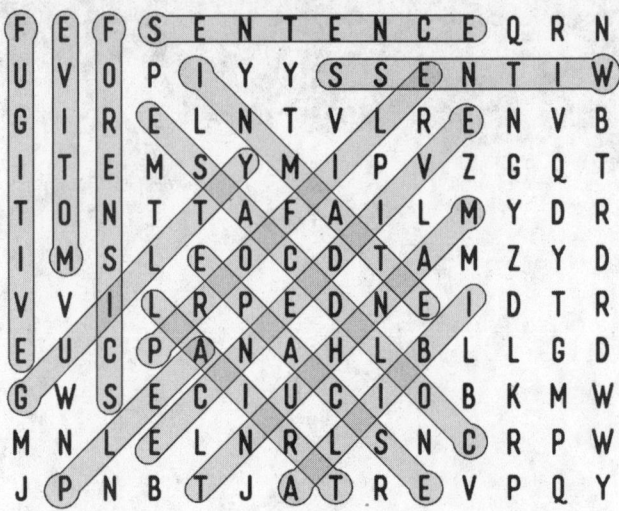

NAMED, YET NEVER CAUGHT

1. Zodiac Killer
2. Boston Strangler
3. Bigfoot Killer
4. Jack the Ripper
5. Texarkana Moonlight Murderer
6. Dr. No
7. Sleepy Hollow Killer
8. Wednesday Strangler
9. The Doodler
10. Alphabet Killer
11. Oklahoma City Butcher
12. Miami Strangler
13. Gold Sock Killer
14. Frankford Slasher

KILLER MOVIES

1. N
2. L
3. D
4. E
5. O
6. M
7. J
8. G
9. B
10. C
11. A
12. I
13. F
14. K
15. H

DAHMER'S REGRETS

"I should have gone to college and gone into real estate and got myself an aquarium, that's what I should have done."

MODUS OPERANDI

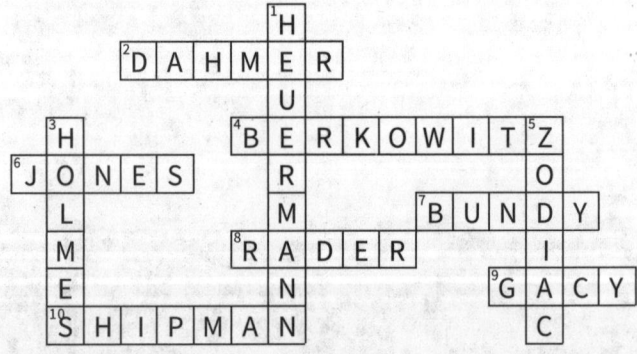

BUNDY'S WORDS OF COMFORT

"What's one less person on the face of the earth, anyway?"

SOLUTIONS

TERRIFYING KILLERS WITH A TYPE
1. AILEEN WUORNOS
2. ANDREI CHIKATILO
3. GLEN ROGERS
4. EDMUND KEMPER
5. JUAN CORONA
6. ALBERT FISH
7. DOROTHEA PUENTE
8. ANDERS BREIVIK
9. TED BUNDY
10. JOJI OBARA
11. ROBERT PICKTON
12. RODNEY ALCALA
13. ROBERT HANSEN
14. CHARLES CULLEN

GACY'S RATIONALE
"Clowns can get away with murder."

THE MOST PROLIFIC AMERICAN KILLERS

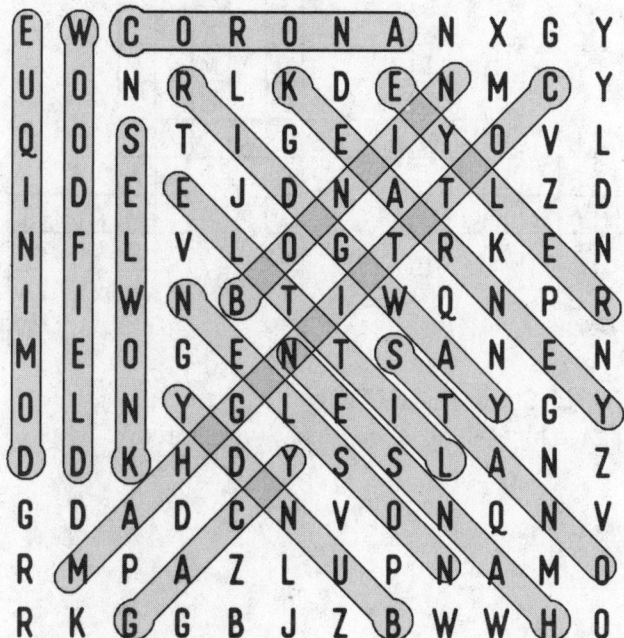

STICKY ENDS
1. M
2. B
3. K
4. A
5. D
6. H
7. E
8. L
9. J
10. G
11. C
12. F
13. N
14. O
15. I

KILLER RECALL
1. AT WORK
2. CLOGGED DRAINS
3. NEGLECT
4. NO
5. LEUKEMIA
6. WRITING LETTERS
7. INSIGHT
8. NONE
9. THE GRAY MAN
10. SOCIAL SECURITY

KILLER PUZZLES

CRIMES OF PASSION
IN THE HEAT OF THE MOMENT

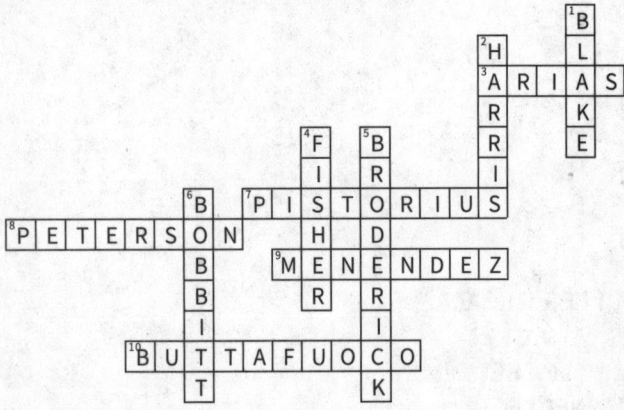

CRIMINAL CONFESSIONS
1. TED BUNDY
2. SAMMY GRAVANO
3. RICHARD SPECK
4. SHEBORAH THOMAS
5. ANDREI CHIKATILO
6. LYLE MENENDEZ
7. OSCAR PISTORIUS
8. JODI ARIAS
9. AILEEN WUORNOS
10. IAN BRADY
11. JOHN WAYNE GACY
12. WILLIAM KORZON
13. GARY RIDGWAY
14. DIANE STAUDTE

TWISTED TOOLS
1. N
2. J
3. M
4. L
5. G
6. O
7. E
8. K
9. I
10. B
11. H
12. D
13. C
14. A
15. F

LORENA'S REASONING
"I tried to drive the car, obviously, but I had this thing in my hand, so I couldn't drive, so I got rid of it."

HOW TO CATCH A KILLER

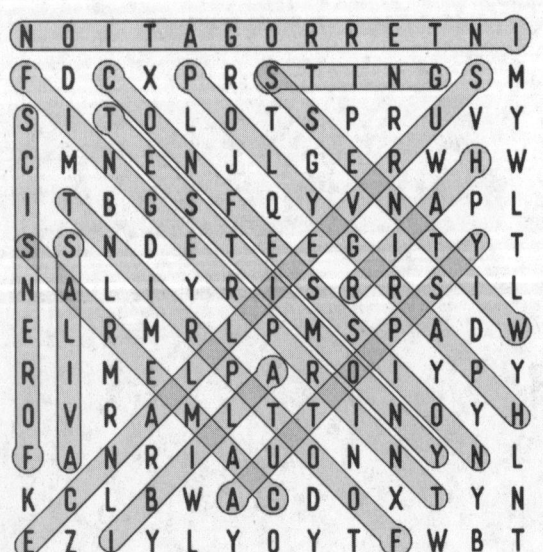

LETHAL LOVE TRIANGLES

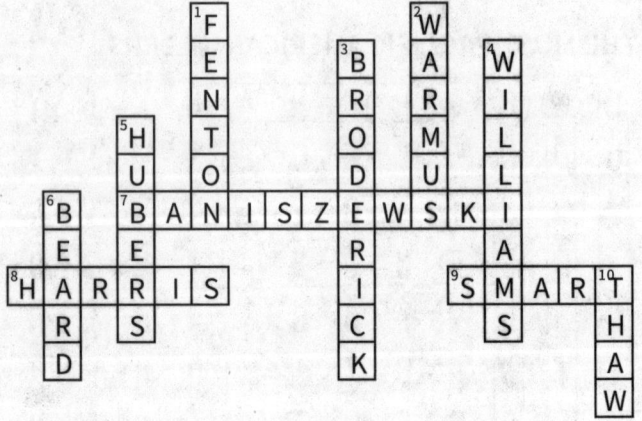

HUBERS'S EXPLANATION
"I gave him the nose job he always wanted."

SOLUTIONS

MAINTAINING THEIR INNOCENCE
1. EDWARD SURRATT
2. IVAN MILAT
3. CARLOS DELUNA
4. RAY KRONE
5. SAM SHEPPARD
6. LEONARD PELTIER
7. DAMIEN ECHOLS
8. AILEEN WUORNOS
9. ADNAN SYED
10. AMANDA KNOX
11. SCOTT PETERSON
12. JEFFREY MACDONALD
13. GARY RIDGWAY
14. MICHAEL PETERSON

HUNTLEY'S MANIPULATION
"It's just dreadful. I just pray that they are alive and well."

CRIME SCENE ESSENTIALS

NOTORIOUS COORDINATES
1. M
2. F
3. O
4. K
5. H
6. B
7. I
8. N
9. G
10. L
11. D
12. J
13. A
14. E
15. C

KILLER RECALL
1. THE CONFESSION KILLER
2. REVOLVER
3. ALASKA
4. FALSE
5. FALLING DOWN THE STAIRS
6. 911 OPERATOR
7. ABUSE
8. NEW YORK
9. OPEN FIELD
10. FORTY-NINE

KILLER PUZZLES

SPIES AND ASSASSINS

SHOTS AT THE OVAL

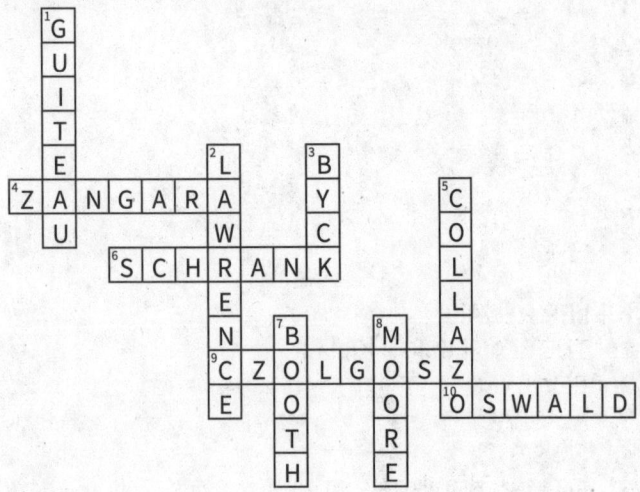

ESPIONAGE HOT SPOTS

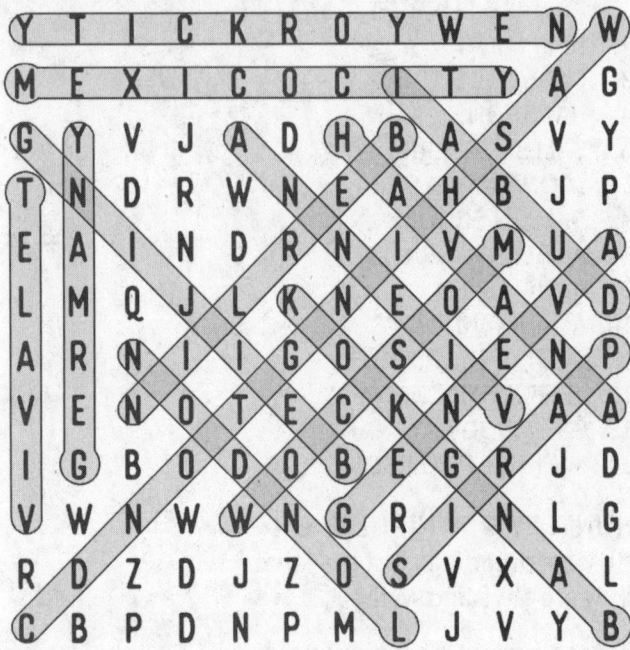

CELEBRITY TARGETS

1. J
2. E
3. N
4. H
5. B
6. M
7. O
8. D
9. K
10. A
11. I
12. C
13. F
14. L
15. G

CHAPMAN'S NOTORIETY

"I knew it was wrong, but I wanted the fame so much that I was willing to give everything and take a human life."

SECRET AGENT SCRAMBLE

1. KLAUS FUCHS
2. OLEG GORDIEVSKY
3. MATA HARI
4. KIM PHILBY
5. ROBERT HANSEN
6. VIKTOR BELENKO
7. JOHN WALKER
8. JUAN PUJOL GARCIA
9. RICHARD SORGE
10. KIM DONG-CHUL
11. ALDRICH AMES
12. KENDALL MYERS
13. JONATHAN POLLARD
14. ANNA CHAPMAN

SOLUTIONS

UNDERCOVER OPERATIONS

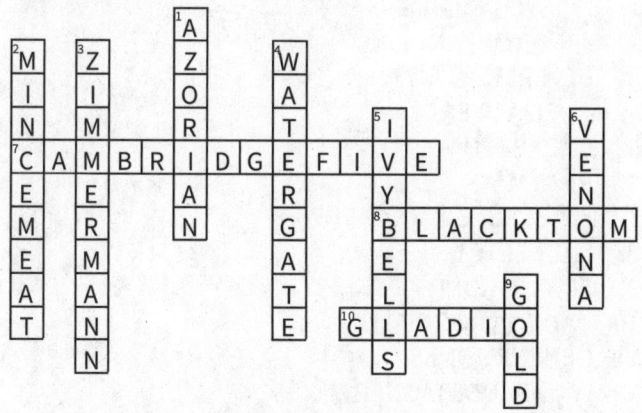

PHILBY'S RATIONALIZATION

"I don't think I was a traitor. I was working for a higher cause."

DECODING SPY GADGETS

1. INVISIBLE INK
2. MICROFILM CAMERA
3. LISTENING DEVICE
4. SIGNAL JAMMER
5. GPS TRACKER
6. SMOKE BOMB
7. LISTENING POST
8. KEYLOGGER
9. FLASHLIGHT CAMERA
10. UNIVERSAL SERIAL BUS (USB)
11. HIDDEN KNIFE
12. MICROPHONE
13. PEN CAMERA
14. NIGHT VISION GOGGLES

HASENFUS'S REALIZATION

"I knew too much, and that made me a liability. Sometimes, knowing the truth is more dangerous than living in ignorance."

NOTABLE TARGETS

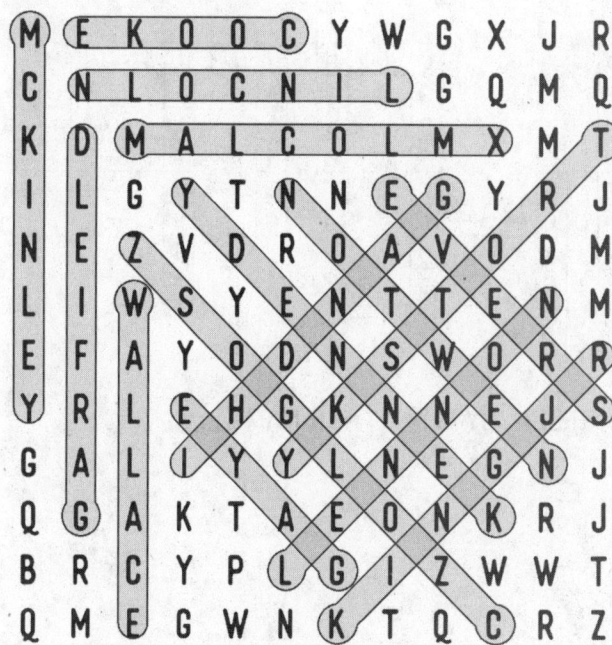

THE ESPIONAGE NETWORK

1. L
2. K
3. O
4. J
5. M
6. B
7. I
8. E
9. G
10. D
11. N
12. F
13. A
14. C
15. H

KILLER RECALL

1. JACKSON
2. THERESA SALDANA
3. FAME
4. TRUE
5. WATERGATE
6. THIRTY YEARS
7. FALSE
8. JUAN PUJOL GARCIA
9. ACOUSTIC KITTY
10. HANDLER

KILLER PUZZLES

FEMME FATALES

MOMMY DEAREST

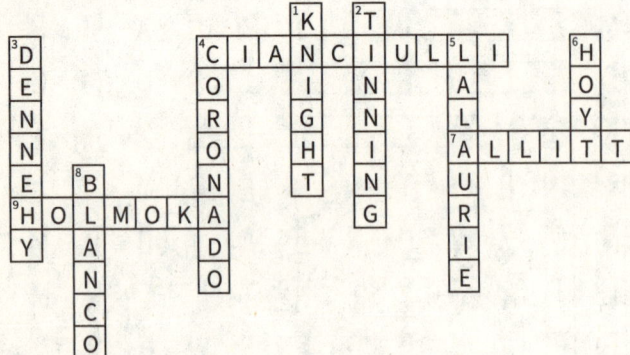

A KILLER, BY ANY OTHER NAME . . .

1. F
2. E
3. O
4. B
5. K
6. A
7. L
8. N
9. M
10. I
11. J
12. D
13. C
14. H
15. G

WUORNOS'S STRANGE END

"I'm sailing with the Rock, and I'll be back, like *Independence Day* with Jesus."

FLIRTING WITH MURDER

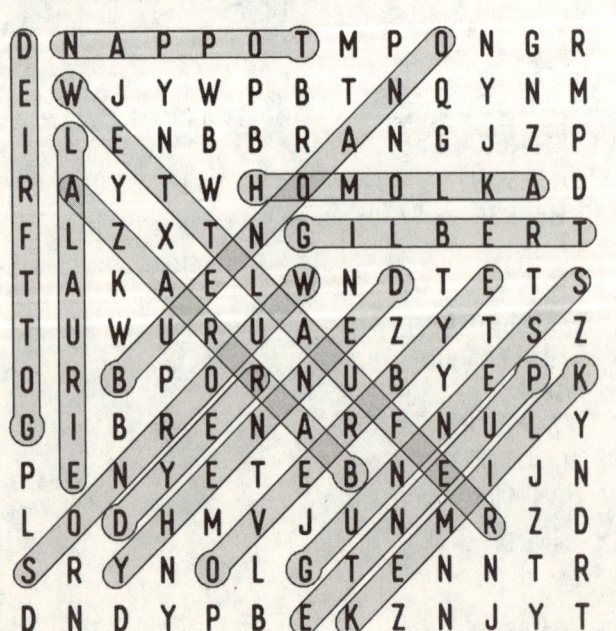

GOODNIGHT NURSE

1. KRISTEN GILBERT
2. JANE TOPPAN
3. BEVERLEY ALLITT
4. AMELIA DYER
5. ELIZABETH WETTLAUFER
6. RETA MAYS
7. KIMBERLY CLARK SAENZ
8. LUCY LETBY
9. AINO NYKOPP-KOSKI
10. DANIELA POGGIALI
11. GENENE JONES
12. WALTRAUD WAGNER
13. LINDA HAZZARD
14. GWENDOLYN GRAHAM

ARSENIC AND OLD LACE

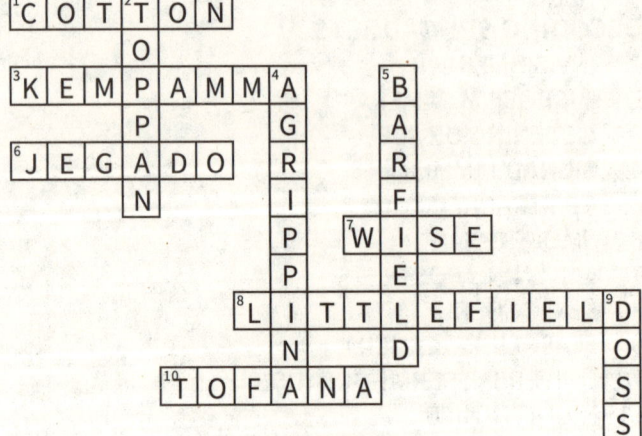

METHODS OF MURDER

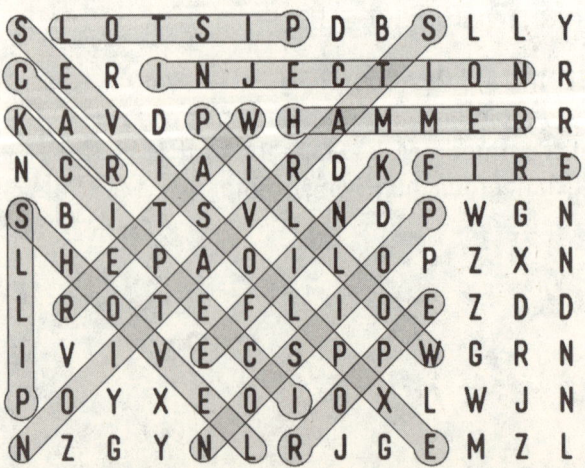

SOLUTIONS

BLACK WIDOWS
1. NANNIE DOSS
2. JUDY BUENOANO
3. GESCHE GOTTFRIED
4. TILLIE KLIMEK
5. AMY ARCHER-GILLIGAN
6. BLANCHE TAYLOR MOORE
7. EVELYN DICK
8. MARY ELIZABETH WILSON
9. BETTY LOU BEETS
10. KATHERINE KNIGHT
11. BELLE GUNNESS
12. BETTY NEUMAR
13. STACEY CASTOR
14. CHISAKO KAKEHI

MURDER FOR MONEY

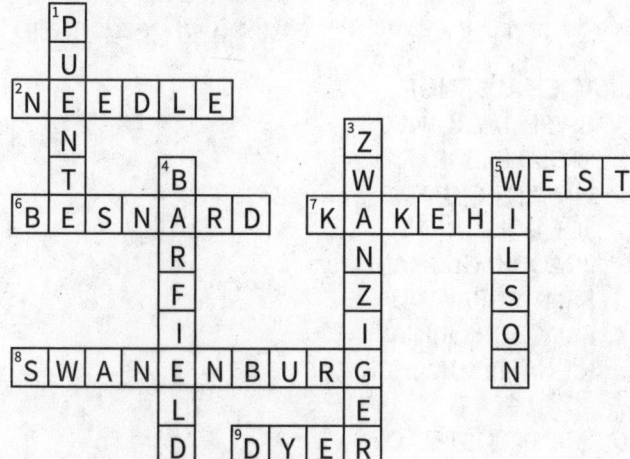

ATKINS'S SOLUTION
"She kept begging and pleading and pleading and begging, and I got sick of listening to her so I stabbed her."

MOTIVES FOR MURDER

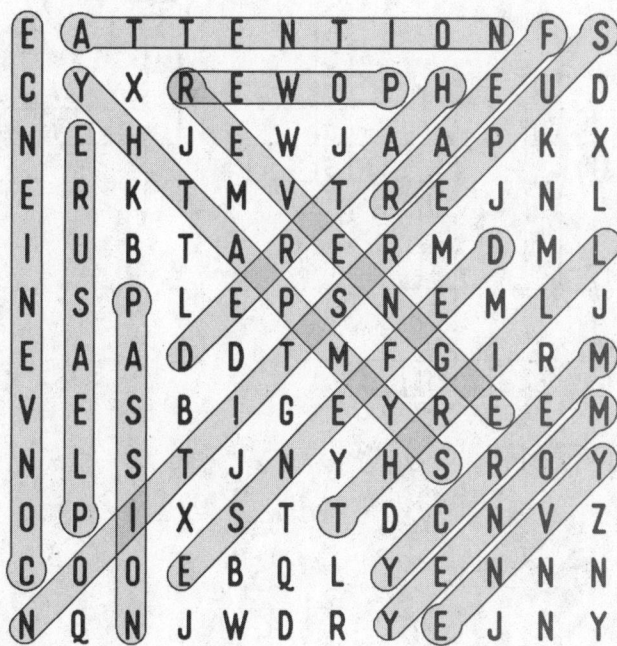

PARTNERS IN CRIME
1. B
2. O
3. M
4. G
5. F
6. H
7. C
8. J
9. L
10. N
11. I
12. E
13. A
14. D
15. K

CIANCIULLI'S CLEAN GETAWAY
"After a long time on the boil, I was able to make some most acceptable creamy soap."

KILLER RECALL
1. RARER
2. SOCIAL SECURITY CHECKS
3. SHARON TATE
4. UNDER THE WISHING WELL
5. SOAP
6. POSTPARTUM PSYCHOSIS
7. MONEY
8. ELIZABETH BÁTHORY
9. KARLA HOMOLKA
10. FORTY-NINE

KILLER PUZZLES

ORGANIZED CRIMES
MOB BOSS MAYHEM

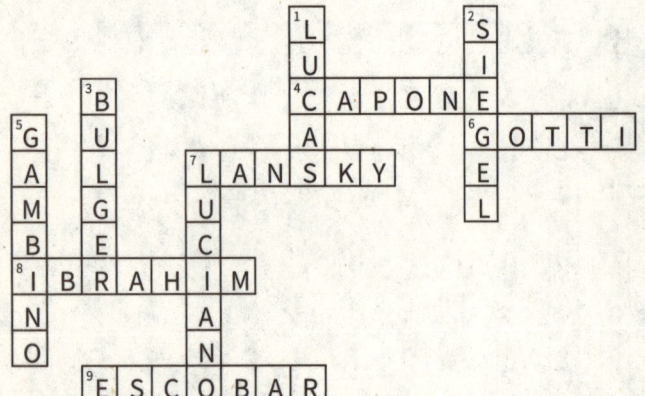

UNDERWORLD ACTIVITIES

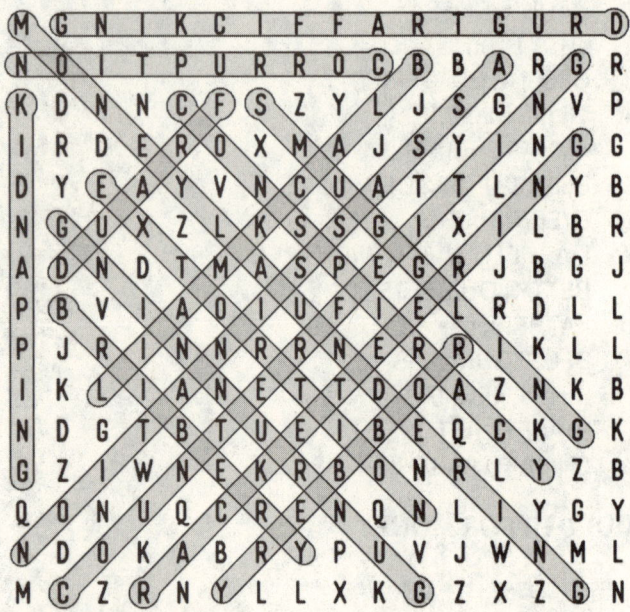

MAFIA MAP
1. O
2. J
3. D
4. C
5. N
6. L
7. K
8. H
9. G
10. B
11. M
12. F
13. I
14. E
15. A

ESCOBAR'S PREFERENCE
"I prefer to be in the grave in Colombia than in a jail cell in the United States."

ALIAS CHALLENGE
1. GRISELDA BLANCO
2. PABLO ESCOBAR
3. VINCENT GIGANTE
4. JOE BONANNO
5. JOAQUIN GUZMAN
6. SAMMY GRAVANO
7. SALVATORE RIINA
8. RICHARD KUKLINSKI
9. JOHN GOTTI
10. FRANK COSTELLO
11. JOEY MERLINO
12. SEMION MOGLIEVICH
13. MARTIN CAHILL
14. CHARLES LUCIANO

SOLUTIONS

GANGSTERS ONSCREEN

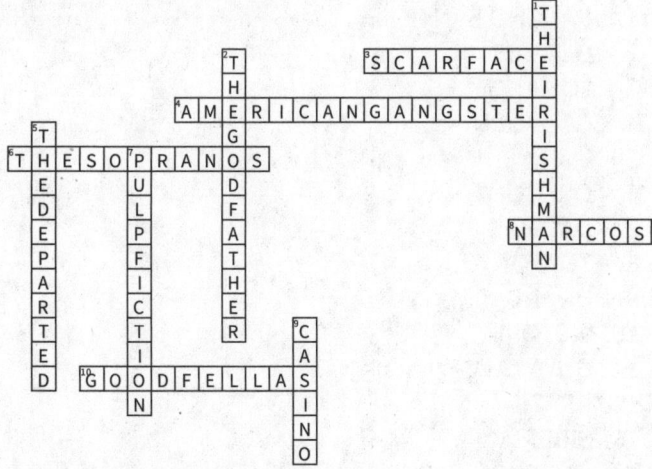

CRACKING DOWN ON CRIME

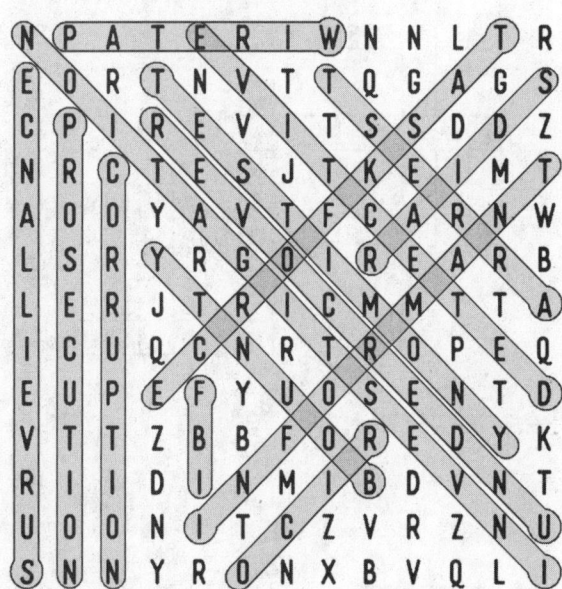

COPPOLA'S WARNING
"Keep your friends close, but your enemies closer."

GRITTY GLOSSARY
1. MOOLAH
2. SNITCH
3. HIT
4. CAPISCE
5. GUMSHOE
6. GOON
7. MOBSTER
8. FUGITIVE
9. PATSY
10. CAPER
11. RAT
12. SHIV
13. DIME
14. TURF

CAPONE'S DEFENSE
"I'm not a monster. I'm a businessman."

MOBSTER METHODS
1. J
2. I
3. G
4. O
5. K
6. N
7. H
8. C
9. B
10. L
11. E
12. A
13. M
14. F
15. D

KILLER RECALL
1. LAS VEGAS
2. CHICAGO
3. TRUE
4. GRISELDA BLANCO
5. FALSE
6. AMERICAN GANGSTER
7. NATIONAL CRIME SYNDICATE
8. BUSINESSMAN
9. SNITCH
10. EL CHAPO

KILLER PUZZLES

CULT KILLINGS

INFAMOUS CULT LEADERS

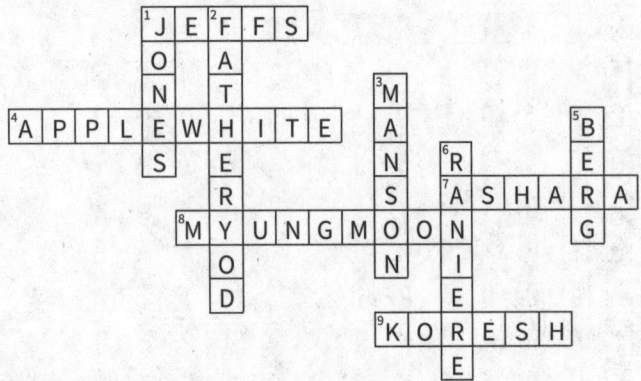

DARK DESTINATIONS
1. RANCHO SANTE FE
2. QUEBEC
3. LOS ANGELES
4. CALIFORNIA
5. LIMA
6. OREGON
7. DAEGU
8. TOKYO
9. UGANDA
10. VICTORIA
11. GUYANA
12. BRAZIL
13. SIBERIA
14. CALIFORNIA

MASTERS OF INFLUENCE
1. E
2. F
3. M
4. O
5. L
6. H
7. J
8. A
9. I
10. C
11. N
12. B
13. K
14. D
15. G

CULT CLASSICS

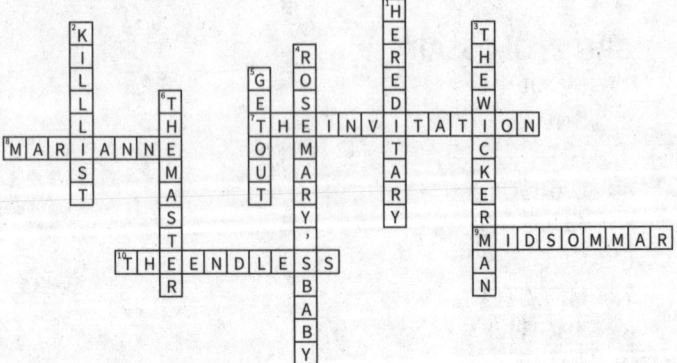

KORESH'S CONCEIT
"I am the way, the truth, and the life. No one comes to the Father except through me."

JONES'S MANIPULATION
"We didn't commit suicide; we committed an act of revolutionary suicide."

SEARCH FOR SECRETS

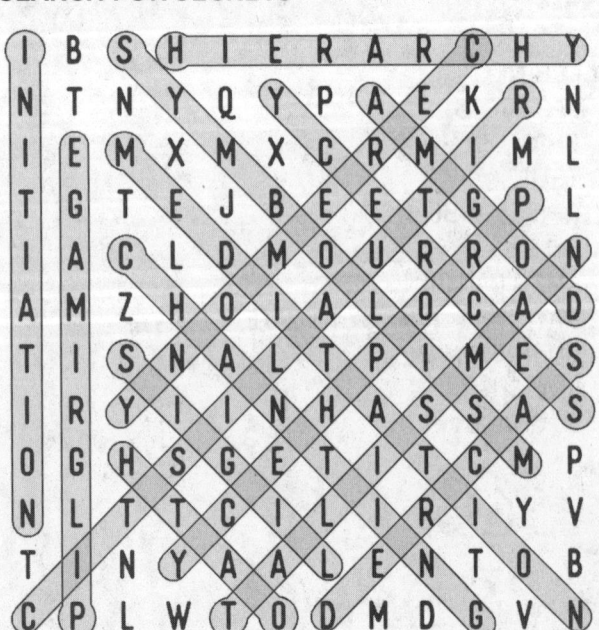

SOLUTIONS

FATAL PROPHECIES
1. HEAVEN'S GATE
2. BRANCH DAVIDIANS
3. AUM SHINRIKYO
4. PEOPLES TEMPLE
5. SOLAR TEMPLE
6. CHURCH OF THE LAST TESTAMENT
7. RAELIAN MOVEMENT
8. CHILDREN OF GOD
9. THE FAMILY
10. MANSON FAMILY
11. THE BIBLE SPEAKS
12. HOUSE OF YAHWEH
13. NEW ALLIANCE
14. UNIFICATION CHURCH

MANSON'S DEFLECTION
"These children that come at you with knives, they are your children. You taught them. I didn't teach them. I just tried to help them stand up."

MIND GAMES

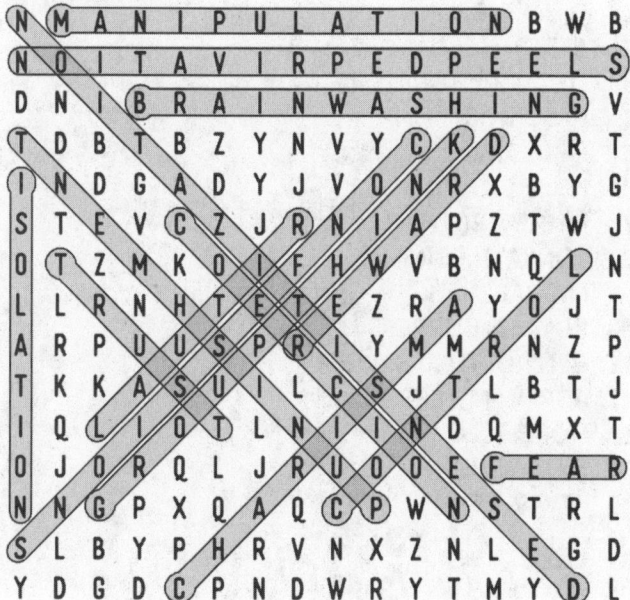

SURVIVOR STORIES
1. J
2. F
3. M
4. L
5. C
6. O
7. G
8. I
9. D
10. H
11. K
12. A
13. N
14. E
15. B

KILLER RECALL
1. DAVID KORESH
2. JONESTOWN
3. TRUE
4. 1994
5. *THE WICKER MAN*
6. MUSICIAN
7. JOAQUIN PHOENIX
8. TRUE
9. HEAVEN'S GATE
10. SHARON TATE

THE DARK SIDE OF FAME

MUSICIANS' TRAGIC ENDS

CIRCUMSTANCES OF DEATH

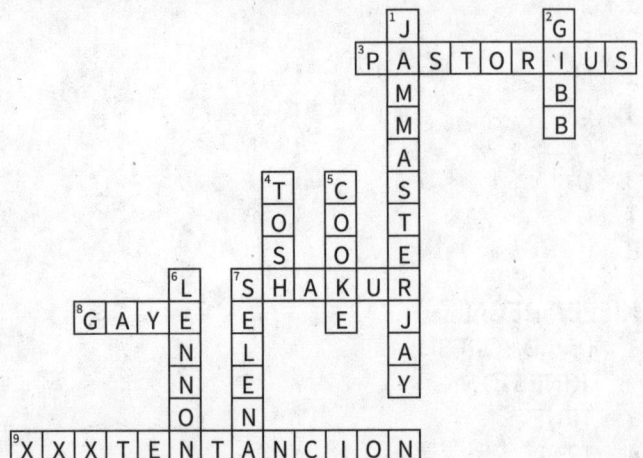
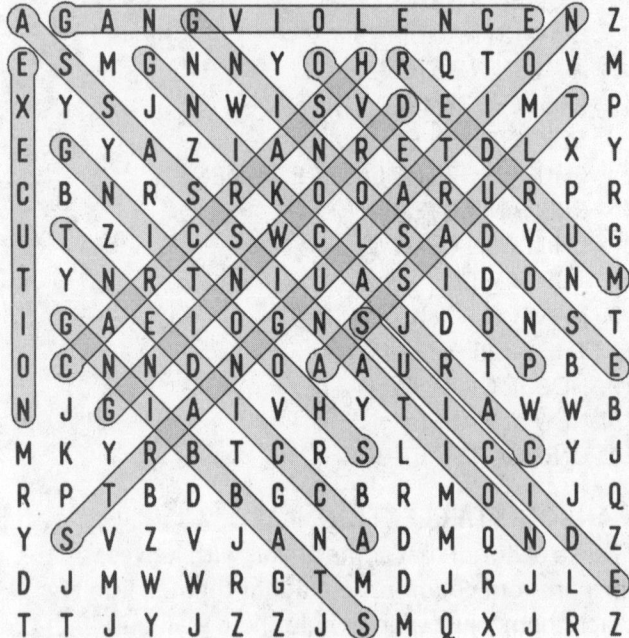

GONE TOO SOON

1. D
2. K
3. F
4. L
5. G
6. N
7. E
8. H
9. J
10. O
11. I
12. A
13. C
14. B
15. M

CHANEL'S REMORSE

"Guilt is perhaps the most painful companion of death."

ATHLETES IN THE HOT SEAT

1. O. J. SIMPSON
2. AARON HERNANDEZ
3. OSCAR PISTORIUS
4. RAY LEWIS
5. MIKE TYSON
6. KOBE BRYANT
7. RAE CARRUTH
8. TONYA HARDING
9. MICHAEL VICK
10. PLAXICO BURRESS
11. BEN ROETHLISBERGER
12. ADRIAN PETERSON
13. HOPE SOLO
14. MARION JONES
15. JAVARIS CRITTENTON

SOLUTIONS

HOLLYWOOD HEISTS

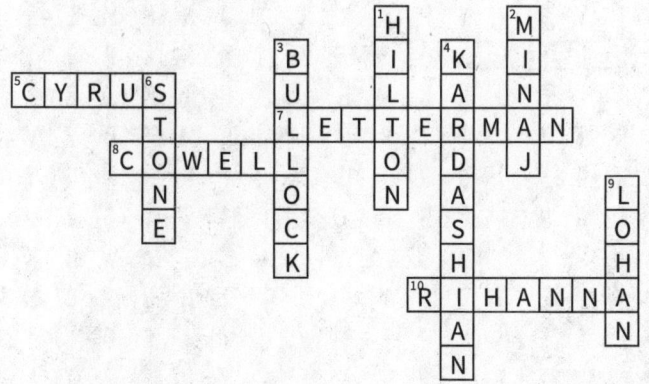

SIMPSON'S SPECULATION

"Let's say I committed this crime . . . even if I did do this, it would have been because I loved her very much, right?"

FALLEN STARS

1. JIM MORRISON
2. ELIZABETH SHORT
3. TUPAC SHAKUR
4. JILL DANDO
5. NATALIE WOOD
6. CHRISTOPHER WALLACE
7. GIANNI VERSACE
8. DOMINIQUE DUNNE
9. LEE MORGAN
10. BRANDON LEE
11. RONNI CHASEN
12. DIMEBAG DARRELL
13. TODD BRIDGES
14. MIA ZAPATA

JACKSON'S IMMORTAL WORDS

"Who wants mortality? Everybody wants immortality. . . . I just want it to live forever and just give all that I have."

PROTECTION METHODS

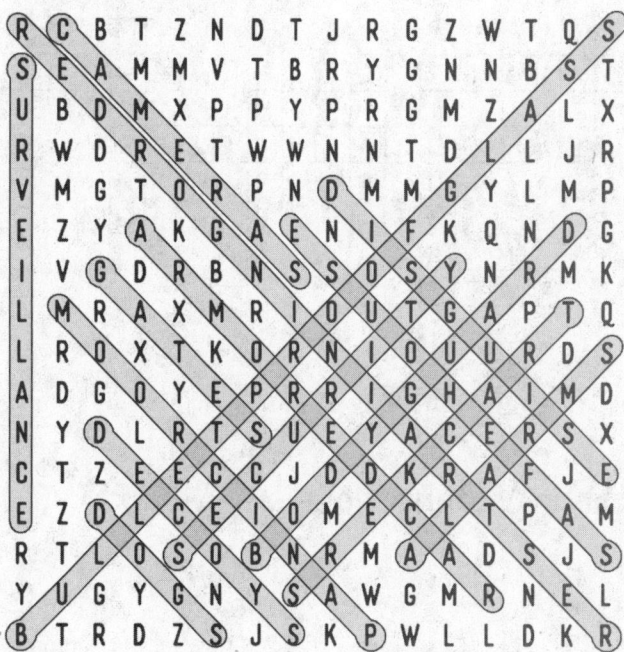

CINEMATIC CRIMINALS

1. D
2. N
3. G
4. K
5. C
6. H
7. O
8. I
9. B
10. J
11. A
12. L
13. E
14. M
15. F

KILLER RECALL

1. HIS FATHER
2. ACUTE PROPOFOL POISONING
3. 1994
4. DOGFIGHTING
5. ALEC
6. TRUE
7. ELIZABETH SHORT
8. TRUE
9. TUPAC
10. "NO, THEY SURE CAN'T."

185

KILLER PUZZLES

HISTORY-MAKING CASES

LEGENDARY LAWBREAKERS

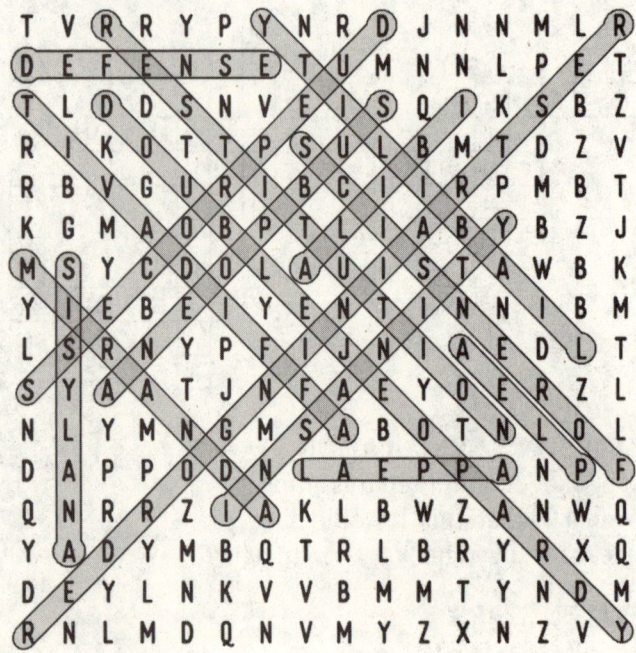

CRIMINAL CONNECTIONS

1. I
2. N
3. K
4. D
5. H
6. M
7. C
8. J
9. A
10. E
11. G
12. O
13. F
14. B
15. L

MANSON'S MOTIVATION

"If you're going to do something, do it well. And leave something witchy."

LEGAL JARGON

SITES OF INFAMY

1. LOS ANGELES
2. DALLAS
3. LONDON
4. CHICAGO
5. MEMPHIS
6. HOPEWELL
7. BOSTON
8. SAN FRANCISCO
9. FLORIDA
10. YORKSHIRE
11. MANCHESTER
12. MIAMI BEACH
13. PLAINFIELD
14. OSLO

SOLUTIONS

CONTROVERSIAL EXECUTIONS

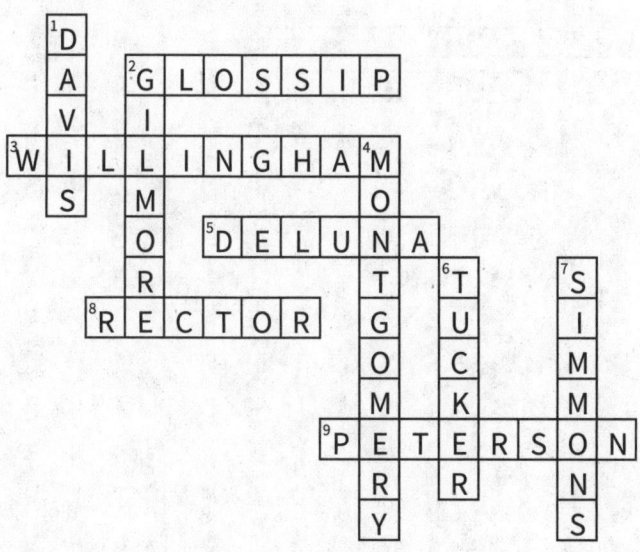

KILLER NICKNAMES

APPEL'S GALLOWS HUMOR
"Well, gentlemen, you are about to see a baked Appel."

EARTH-SHATTERING CRIMES
1. JFK ASSASSINATION
2. LINDBERGH BABY KIDNAPPING
3. BOSTON MARATHON BOMBING
4. JONBENÉT RAMSEY
5. CASEY ANTHONY
6. HEAVEN'S GATE
7. LUKA MAGNOTTA
8. OKLAHOMA CITY BOMBING
9. SANDY HOOK
10. UNIVERSITY OF WASHINGTON
11. SEPTEMBER ELEVENTH
12. TED BUNDY
13. MALCOLM X
14. COLUMBINE SHOOTING

RADER'S REASONING
"I actually think I may be possessed with demons; I was dropped on my head as a kid."

MASTERS OF ESCAPE
1. D
2. K
3. M
4. C
5. J
6. G
7. H
8. L
9. I
10. F
11. A
12. E
13. B
14. O
15. N

KILLER RECALL
1. FALSE
2. COURTHOUSE WINDOW
3. MOVIE THEATER
4. THE BEACH BOYS
5. CHICAGO
6. GIANNI VERSACE
7. TRUE
8. SEVENTEEN
9. THE LINDBERGH LAW
10. BIND, TORTURE, KILL

KILLER PUZZLES

SHOCKING STALKERS

MILESTONES IN STALKING PREVENTION

PSYCHOLOGICAL PROFILES

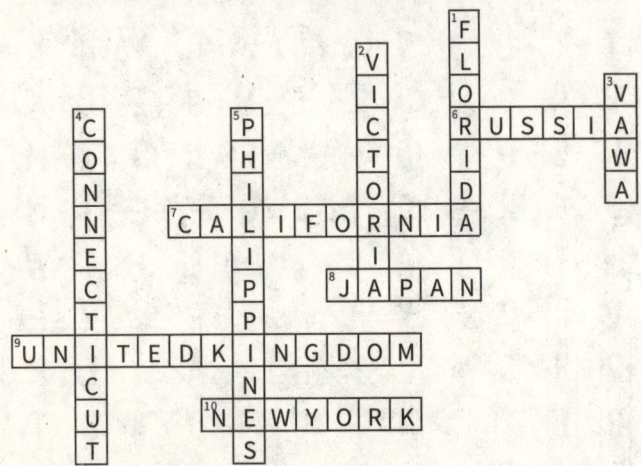

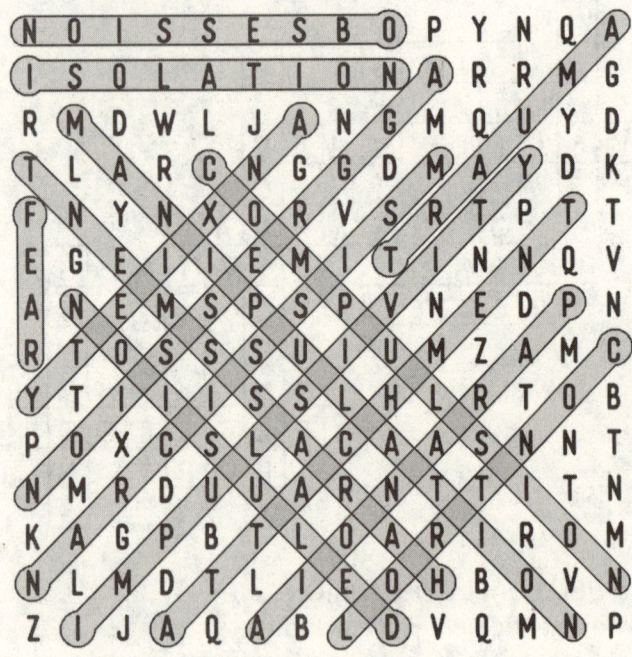

LEGAL BOUNDARIES

1. B
2. A
3. F
4. K
5. M
6. C
7. I
8. O
9. G
10. L
11. D
12. J
13. E
14. N
15. H

CORBETT'S DELUSION

"I love you and you are very special to me. And without you in my life, there is only misery."

FAME AND FEAR

1. REBECCA SCHAEFFER
2. DEMI LOVATO
3. JODIE FOSTER
4. TINA TURNER
5. MADONNA
6. JOHN LENNON
7. KRISTEN STEWART
8. SCARLETT JOHANSSON
9. MILEY CYRUS
10. MICHAEL J FOX
11. JUSTIN BIEBER
12. TAYLOR SWIFT
13. SHERYL CROW
14. EVAN RACHEL WOOD
15. SELENA GOMEZ

FATAL OBSESSIONS

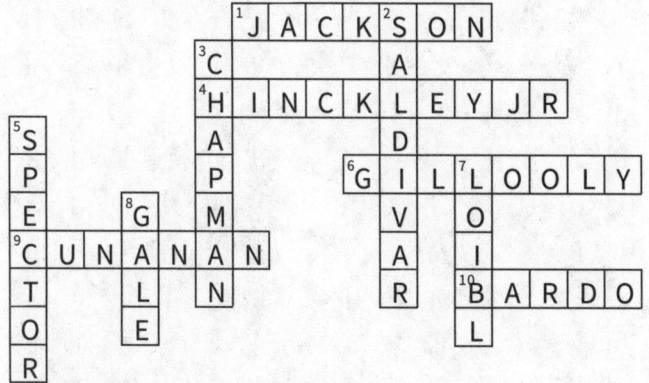

GRASSO'S LAST GROUSE
"I did not get my Spaghetti-O's; I got spaghetti. I want the press to know this."

NAMING NAMES
1. YOLANDA SALDÍVAR
2. ROBERT JOHN BARDO
3. MARGARET MARY RAY
4. JOHN HINCKLEY, JR.
5. MARK DAVID CHAPMAN
6. ARTHUR JACKSON
7. JOSHUA CORBETT
8. RICARDO LÓPEZ
9. ROBERT DEWEY HOSKINS
10. MARK REVILL
11. ROBERT O'RYAN
12. DANTE MICHAEL SOIU
13. THOMAS BRODNICKI
14. BRETT FORSELL

MAUDSLEY'S DEFENSE
"I believe I was doing my victims a favor. They needed to be freed from this world."

SUPPORT FOR VICTIMS

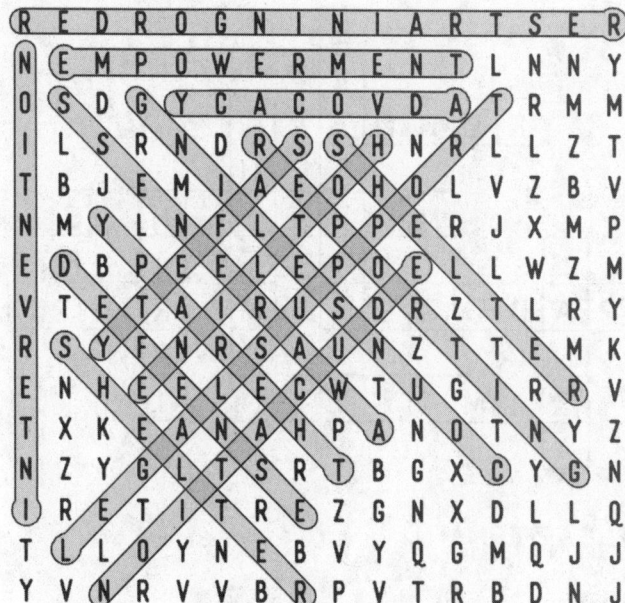

POP CULTURE PREDATORS
1. E
2. F
3. J
4. L
5. A
6. B
7. O
8. I
9. H
10. N
11. K
12. D
13. M
14. C
15. G

KILLER RECALL
1. CALIFORNIA
2. BUNNY
3. EMOTIONAL DISTRESS
4. TRUE
5. JODIE FOSTER
6. MARGARET MARY RAY
7. ARTHUR JACKSON
8. FALSE
9. ROBERT JOHN MAUDSLEY
10. *FATAL ATTRACTION*

MASS MURDERERS

NAMES BEHIND THE HEADLINES

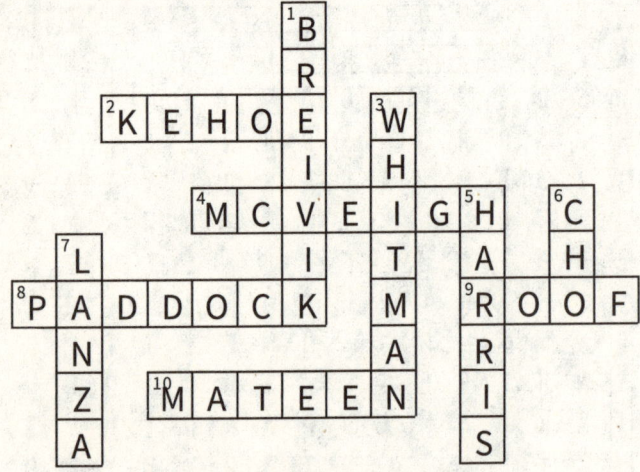

PUBLIC REACTION

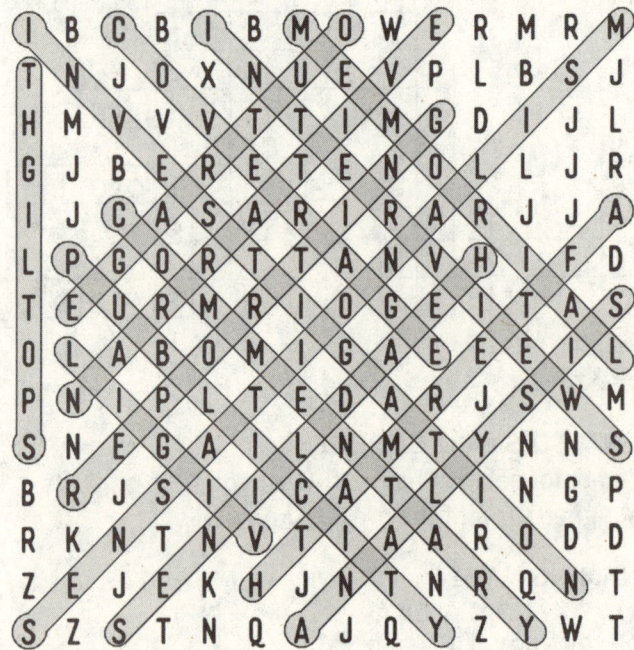

THE AFTERMATH

1. O
2. N
3. C
4. E
5. F
6. G
7. D
8. I
9. J
10. H
11. K
12. L
13. M
14. B
15. A

CHO'S JUSTIFICATION

"You forced me into a corner. You didn't understand me."

UNDER THE RADAR

1. ROBERT HAWKINS
2. CARL BROWN
3. HUAN YUN XIANG
4. COLIN FERGUSON
5. PATRICK SHERRILL
6. ANDREAS LUBITZ
7. OMAR THORN
8. SCOTT DEKRAAI
9. ROBERT DEAR
10. ARCAN CETIN
11. FRANCISCO PAULA GONZALES
12. BYRAN UYESUGI
13. ELLIOT RODGER
14. TRAVIS REINKING

NOTHING NEW

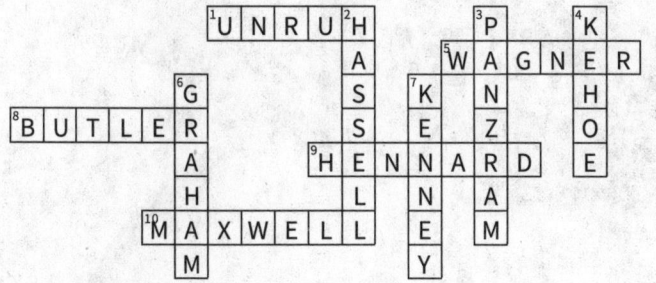

MCVEIGH'S PHILOSOPHY
"I am the master of my fate; I am the captain of my soul."

SITES OF HORROR
1. BOULDER
2. BURLINGTON
3. CHARLESTON
4. LITTLETON
5. SUTHERLAND SPRINGS
6. SPRINGFIELD
7. UTØYA ISLAND
8. ORLANDO
9. AURORA
10. SAN YSIDRO
11. CHRISTCHURCH
12. KENYA, TANZANIA
13. EL PASO
14. PITTSBURGH

HARRIS AND KLEBOLD'S GOALS
"Directors will be fighting over this story. I know we're gonna have followers because we're so f*cking God-like."

NO REGRETS

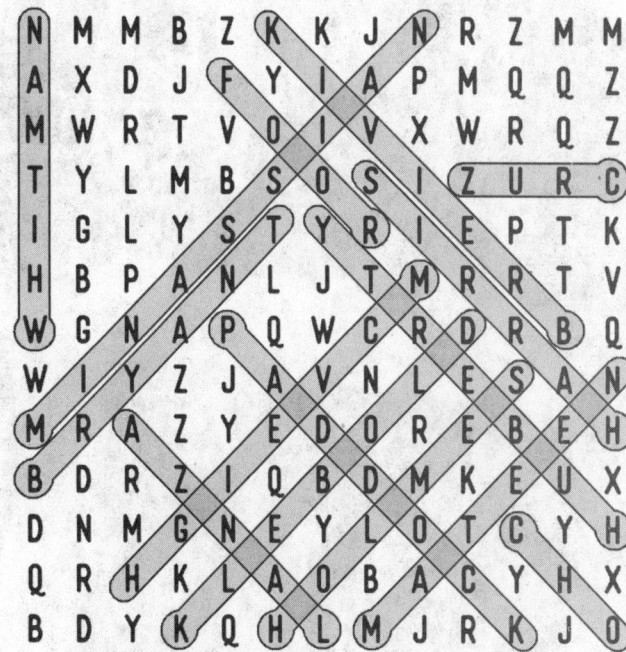

PROFILES IN CRIMINALITY
1. I
2. B
3. M
4. H
5. G
6. F
7. N
8. K
9. A
10. J
11. E
12. C
13. H
14. D
15. L

KILLER RECALL
1. BREIVIK
2. MENTAL HEALTH AWARENESS
3. SANDY HOOK
4. JACK GILBERT GRAHAM
5. AURORA
6. 30 PERCENT
7. TRUE
8. ORLANDO
9. FALSE
10. SCHIZOTYPAL PERSONALITY DISORDER

IF YOU'RE A TRUE TRUE CRIME FAN...

CHECK OUT THESE OTHER BOOKS!

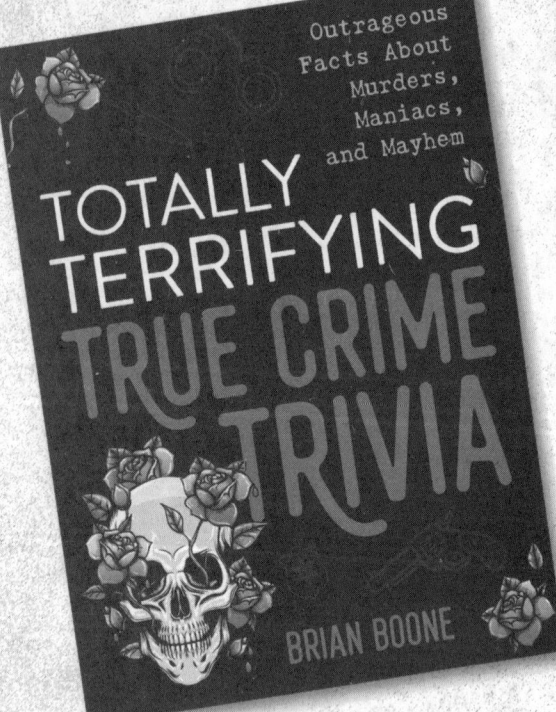